LIVING
Single

THE DIFFERENT FACES OF
SINGLENESS

Kervin J. Smith

LIVING SINGLE: The Different Faces of Singleness

ISBN: 0-924748-46-X
UPC: 88571300016-1

Printed in the United States of America
© 2005 by Kervin Smith

Milestones International Publishers
4410 University Dr., Ste. 113
Huntsville, AL 35816
(256) 536-9402, ext. 234; Fax: (256) 536-4530
www.milestonesinternationalpublishers.com

1 2 3 4 5 6 7 8 9 10 11 / 10 09 08 07 06 05

Kervin J. Smith has written a masterpiece! His insightfulness and thorough research on "living single" while being saved is phenomenal. This book must be read by every single and parent in the body of Christ.

Gary Hawkins
Sr. Pastor, Voices of Faith Ministries
Stone Mountain, Georgia

Kervin J. Smith courageously tackles the issues that are confronting single Christians and their sexuality today. He unfolds jaw-jarring truths that will give breakthrough power for many single ministries.

Pastor Jerone L. Davison
Founder/Pastor, Bountiful Harvest Church
Fairfield, California
Former NFL Player,
San Francisco 49ers and Oakland Raiders

John 8:32 (KJV) says, *"Ye shall know the truth, and the truth shall make you free."* The only way to get free is hearing and doing the truth (the Word of God). This book is a "must read" for anyone living single and desiring to walk in God's best.

Dr. Bernard Grant
Showers of Blessing Christian Center
Rocky Mount, North Carolina

If you've never been married or are divorced or widowed, this book may be the most significant and life-impacting piece of literature you'll read for some time to come! Dr.

Smith addresses a sensitive and sometimes controversial subject with tactful wisdom and insightful humor that will most certainly encourage the single man or woman that God has a divine plan that will not be thwarted by counterfeits, compromises, or carnal inclinations!

In light of the current state of relationships, the overwhelming bombardment of shifting definitions of male/female roles, and the cultural attacks on marriage, this timely tome will prove to be prophetic in the strategies it offers to the body of Christ, whether married or single! Essential reading.

Dr. Robert L. Bryan, Jr.
Sword of the Spirit Ministry
Forestville, Maryland

If there is ever a time when singles need direction on how to successfully live single, it is now. Kervin J. Smith in *Living Single* shows the clear-cut blueprint to chart the pathway that will end the humdrum of being alone. He articulately explains how singles can once again reclaim the joy, honor, and value of being single. Every *single* person should read this book.

Jack Coe
Jack Coe Ministries
Dallas, Texas

Kervin Smith is a true master. He understands what it takes to lead a successful single life, and in *Living Single* he puts all the key elements together in one place for the rest of the world to see.

John Blumenthal
The Blumenthal Group

Page for page, the best book I have read on singles. Get ready for the ride of your life. I couldn't put it down.

Dr. Stanley M. Williams
Fire of the Word Ministries

Kervin J. Smith presents an eloquent and passionate, thought-provoking tool for all singles. For many years to come this reading will serve as a guide-map for successful dating, relating, and enduring for all singles who desire to do it God's way.

Tiffany Rick Blakeney
J.D., Ph.D.

Dr. Smith has proven to be a SINGLE man of integrity. So it is no wonder that he would embark upon this challenge to bring the unadulterated truth to Christian singles everywhere. In a day when compromise is so prevalent, it takes only one voice to dispel and expose the deceit of the enemy. Kervin Smith is one of those voices. He is anointed by God and called for this time! SINGLES, hear the word of the Lord! And after you have heard the word, OBEY and become the next voice to proclaim what thus saith the Lord. Victorious singleness is not a catch phrase—it is your calling!

Reverend Cliff Lovick
Malachi House
Greensboro, North Carolina

It's exciting to get the perspective of dating from a male's point of view. Dr. Smith is a man of integrity with a lot of insight into dating and singleness. This book is guaranteed to be a powerful tool for men and women living the single life as Christians.

Cassandra Evans
Business Analyst, Asst. Vice President

This book is a must-have for anyone who is purposing to keep the faith in your godly walk with life's circumstances.

Sharon Kirkley
United States Government

This is not just a book to singles; rather, it is a guide to fulfilling destiny and purpose. It will challenge you to make a paradigm shift in your view of just being single to a state of single blessedness.

Alberta Huston
CEO
Bay Area Dream Homes

Finally, a book that lives up to what it claims. *Living Single* really does take your life to the next level and helps you appreciate being single. Using the principles that Dr. Smith has made available to you, you will attain amazing achievement.

Professor Ricardo Caldwell
University of Virgin Islands

This book will definitely ignite a drive in singles to fulfill their purpose in life as they discover their God-given significance and abilities to inherit in the image of God.

Dr. Otis Lockett
Evangel Church

ACKNOWLEDGMENTS

———⟶⟩●⟨⟵———

Aaron Lewis, my friend. I appreciate you for your editorial insights, emotional support, enthusiastic encouragement, and authentic friendship. I admire your integrity and your commitment to excellence.

Nikki Braun, who designed the book cover. I love it!

Jim Rill, without whose Herculean efforts this book would have never been completed. Thank you for your support, insights, and endless production of written words down into a manageable manuscript.

To all of my family and friends for their love, support, and understanding during what has been unquestionably an arduous challenge of my career. Thank you for your incredible patience!

I also want to acknowledge the following important people:

Parthenia Buford	Platinum Member
Laurice A. Simmonds	Platinum Member
Pastor Doug and Ingrid Thompson	Platinum Member
Phyllis Allen	Gold Member
Lisa Kenney-ufere	Gold Member
Nancy Person	Gold Member
Fenton Rhaney	Gold Member
Judi Rodgers	Gold Member
Beauty for Ashes World Outreach Inc.	Gold Member

CONTENTS

INTRODUCTION

———⟫⟪———

As I travel around the country preaching and teaching and inspiring thousands of lives I can't help but notice a strange relational crisis that has brooded among the saints. It goes something like this. People who are married often wish and fantasize about being single all over again. I've literally heard married people say, "If I could only do it all over again, I'd stay single so much longer. When I got married, I was far too young. If only I knew then what I know now…life would sure be different." Yeah, yeah, yeah.

On the flip side I hear a saddening bellyaching from single saints complaining about how unhappy they are living the single life. "I sure wish God would hurry up and send me a husband. I can't stand being alone. Why is it that I have to endure this pain so long? This is torture, and my biological clock is near broken. If God doesn't do something and do it in a hurry, I'm going to lose it. I really hate being single." Whatever! After hearing both the married people who want to be single complaining and the single folks who really want to be married miserably moaning, I'm not sure exactly what's going on.

You may have heard both stories before, from both singles and married couples. In fact, I would feel pretty safe speculating that most single people couldn't care less whether they hear about the downside of married life, witness marital abusiveness in various forms, or are continually warned about a potentially hazardous and life-wrecking partner. They don't care how much you tell them about the benefits of being single; they still feel as if something is missing when they are not married.

So the bottom line is that they are still going to find somebody (no matter who that person is) to marry them. And that's exactly what they do. It does not matter what qualifications that somebody has. The person doesn't have to have a certain appearance. He is not required to hold down a decent paying job. It doesn't matter whether she is short, tall, fat, or anorexic.

That somebody could have a credit rating worse than Satan's and a criminal record longer than Charles Manson's, but those things don't matter as long as the person is available. Rarely will a single person ask questions about familial backgrounds in an effort to discover if there has ever been any horrific behavior that was passed down from one generation to the next. Worse yet, it really does not matter whether that somebody believes in God or not.

These desperate singles just find someone to marry them, and then months later they divorce over the issues already resident in their spouse that they refused to acknowledge when they first met him or her. Or, if they choose to remain married to the person with the lengthy list of issues, they live in the most miserable state of existence, hiding the real truth that the exchange was really not worth it at all. That is what happens after the fact. It's sad to say that, before that happens, no one in the world can talk the lonely single person into staying single and learning how to enjoy the process.

One thing I do know is that both the complaining married person and the moaning lonely single are pretty confused. Another thing I know is that the enemy, who is the author of confusion, has done a pretty good job of causing this emotional disarray. It is God's purpose, plan, and desire for a married couple to enjoy marriage on such a high level that the onlooker should be able to instantly perceive that they are happy and content. The single person needs to exude this same spirit of happiness from being single.

In our day and age the world has made more people confused concerning both sides of this topic. The world makes marriage seem like slavery with all the trappings of shackles, chains, and slave quarters. Equally as confusing is that society makes it seem as if something is wrong with the person who chooses to remain single and finds contentment therein. The male person who desires to stay single is often questioned about his sexuality. He is asked questions such as, "Are you gay? Do you even like women? What's wrong with you?" "You're so strange," people will say just because the person prefers to enjoy being single and contented.

The reason I wrote this book is to settle the score and to shut the mouth of the accuser. I wrote this book as an ode to single people worldwide. Being single myself, I know firsthand just how much society likes to label and group singles with its false stereotypes. The world puts all of us singles into a lonely, forlorn box, place that box neatly on a shelf, and do not use it until they (society) can figure out a way to profit financially from us. Personally, I am a bit bothered by this procedure.

So to dispel society's unfair tactics I've created a new manifesto for singles: *I'm living single and loving it.* Just say it so you will begin to get a feel of how good it is to be single. I realize that you've been somewhat tainted by this worldly system, so you may have to say it out loud a few times before you actually catch on to it and it becomes real to you.

In *Living Single* I am going to dispel all the false notions about being single, de-mystify the age-old secrets, and introduce to you an entirely different way of thinking about single life. You may have thought you were bound before reading this book. But after you have read this book you will be free to fly like an eagle uninhibited by any obstacles, enjoying your life the way God intended for you to do. And by the way, although it may sound like a really liberating idiom, "The sky is not the limit." There are no limits. Once you've received that truth into your spirit, *Living Single* will become heaven on earth, the way God originally planned for life to be.

Chapter One

IS IT REALLY POSSIBLE TO LOVE LIVING SINGLE?

⟶⟶►◆◄⟵

Just reading the title of this chapter somewhat scares me since I am the one who volunteered to deal with the possibility of loving living single. Perhaps one of the first things that I must do before I can teach you how to love living single is unteach you the negative things you have been taught throughout your entire life about being single. At first you may think that "the bug" hasn't really infected you. You may really believe that you have a completely tamper-resistant, disinfected, pure, unaffected opinion about living single.

In fact, you may even believe that you have a very healthy view about single life. Perhaps you do have a clear view on single life. Nonetheless, your view on living single—no matter how sterilized you may think it is—isn't really as clean as you think. Actually, there is really no such thing as a genuine, society-free opinion about anything. The very nature of an opinion comprises other people's opinions to make up the whole.

There is really no such thing as a genuine, society-free opinion about anything.

For the most part everything that you think about on a daily basis is a direct reflection of what you have been hearing other people within your circle say over the years. Even if you don't pay real close attention to what's being said, you will still inevitably be adversely affected by simply hearing what other people are saying about being single without even realizing it. Just hearing those negative things will have a lasting effect on you if you hear them long enough.

Have you ever watched the six o'clock news? If you have, let me inform you that the sole purpose and objective of the news commentators is to influence how you think. You may have thought that their purpose was to report accurate and up-to-date information. Although that is what they may tell you, it's simply not true. They do a stellar job with manipulating how you think.

They influence you on whom to vote for, on whether or not he or she is a worthwhile candidate. They tell you what kind of car to drive. They tell you when you should sell your car based on rumors about recalls and safety features. They dictate what kind of clothing and apparel you should choose based on styles, fads, seasons, and what famous person, actor, or sports figure is endorsing a particular clothing product.

Added to that, with all the constant reports of murders and violence they strategically teach you that you should live in a perpetual state of fear. Taking a step further, they teach you exactly which classification of people and which ethnic group to actually fear the most. After the horrible terrorist attack on September 11, 2001, in New York City, I watched how the newscasters provoked millions of Americans through fear and their power of influence to purchase duct tape to secure their homes with plastic to protect themselves from the possibility of nuclear activity.

It is quite obvious that there has not been a nuclear attack against America. And even if there were, what would duct tape and plastic do to prevent a nuclear spillover? Let me answer that for you. Absolutely nothing! But that did not stop the die-hard followers from obeying the voices of the six o'clock prophets of doom and destruction. It didn't stop the people from buying so much duct tape that the stock in duct tape went soaring through the roof. Regardless of the issue, they work a tough job on most unguarded minds, ultimately manipulating people's worldview.

They don't only work in the areas of politics, religion, purchases, and sports, however; they also work in the area of relationships. They make you feel either really good or absolutely horrible about your single life. The latter is most common. Because of that, my objective is to offer you new alternatives to how you used to think. I once again want to glorify, properly dress, and embellish single life. After all, God enjoys a single's life, why shouldn't you? Now that you understand I have a job to do, let's get right to it.

Before I can teach you how to love your single life, though, I need to deal with the conventional reasons that influenced people's minds to believe negative reports about single living in the first place. There is no sense in trying to treat a problem if we have not first dealt with its root causes. If we do not effectively deal with the root cause of a problem, no matter how much neurological pesticide we spray, the choking weeds are bound to spring back up all over again.

THE HUMDRUM OF BEING SINGLE

I've always wondered why so many single people simply hate single living. If you look around, everything and everybody is geared to making single people feel strange for being single. There are multi-million-dollar dating businesses whose primary job is to get single people hooked up. They skillfully impose the mind-set that something must be wrong with you if you don't have a "man" or a "woman." They prey upon the millions of single people in America who feel regularly lousy at not having someone to spend every waking minute of their day with.

Their innocent and not-so-innocent victims are the millions of people who have literally bought into a lie. They have bought the lie that if you are single you will inevitably experience gross loneliness. I personally know both men and women who have been married for many years and have children from that union, yet who still feel lonely. The truth is that you don't have to have a person in your face every single moment to cure you from loneliness.

What you really need is something constructive to do. Discover your inner talents and abilities. You need to find a productive project or interest to invest your time into. When you give of yourself in a selfless manner, you won't have any time to feel lonely. You can become actively involved in your local church, volunteer in your community, or join a club (not a nightclub) or civic organization.

When you give of yourself in a selfless manner, you won't have any time to feel lonely.

Believe me when I tell you that when you give of yourself to make a difference in the life of another person, not only will it make you feel absolutely incredible about yourself, but you also won't have time to get lonely because you are doing so much. That's right, it takes time—sometimes too much time—on a person's hands to create the environment that leads to loneliness.

Concerning these wise business gurus, not only do these people attempt to make you as a single feel lonely, but they also falsely make you believe that if you don't have a significant other, something must be wrong with you. Perhaps you are not attractive enough or something like that. They literally inundate you with mail, email, door hangers, and free offers enticing you to sign up so you can start being "normal." They use so many different means and they are so relentless in their pursuit that eventually most singles give in to the pressure.

While I was traveling via plane back home from Charlotte, North Carolina, I opened up a magazine published monthly by Northwest Airlines for its frequent flyers to read and enjoy while flying. I could not help but notice a full-page advertisement that told the story of how a young man decided to quit his lucrative law profession to open up a matchmaking dating service. It seemed somewhat strange to me. I thought, *Wait a minute, why would a lawyer stop practicing law to deal with a bunch of singles?*

It's more than likely that this former law student had a bunch of student loans to repay after graduating from his ivy-league school. Added to that, criminal law and litigation has always paid pretty big bucks. After two or three years of practicing law, this young aspiring counselor would have earned himself a pretty wonderful wage affording him a far above average lifestyle. He would easily be able to afford a 5,000-square foot home with a four-car garage, and own or lease a late model Mercedes Benz and Lexus.

He would have a handsome salary affording him the privilege of eating out at the finest restaurants in town, wearing custom-tailored clothing, and traveling to the most exotic spots in the world. Again, I asked myself, *Why would he leave all this to deal with a bunch of low self-esteem, looking for love in all the wrong places, directed and misdirected, searching singles?* Then, just like that, it hit me.

There is only one thing that lawyers want more than money—MORE MONEY. And this young lawyer knew that he would rake in far more profits by dealing with single people in search of other single people, than he would earn from alleged felons trying to get off the hook. After he started his business, it became an overnight multi-million-dollar success. As a result, he never went back to practicing law. Obviously, he did not have to. He made more money from his singles' dating service in one year than he would make from his law profession in ten years.

His business was housed in a contemporarily styled office, where his clientele could come and meet their potential partners face to face. Although this concept of business continues to produce great amounts of revenues, an even larger avenue of revenue comes from the online dating services. There are literally hundreds of millions of people who log on to the worldwide web every single day looking for some product or service. Many people who surf the web are singles, and skilled marketers know exactly how to turn their casual surfing time into big bucks for them.

There are experts who suggest that the future of online dating services will continue to grow despite the massive amounts of steadily growing competition. In fact, competition usually forces companies to use more innovative methods to raise revenues to underwrite their websites, as a result financially benefiting the consumer. The point is that there is not and perhaps will never be a shortage of single people in the world, making them (singles) a highly favored market.

So nearly everywhere you look—in a magazine on the airplane, in your mailbox, on an Internet pop-up screen, on a billboard, or even on a television commercial—you can be sure to find an advertisement strategically written to draw single people into the advertiser's world. Their hype is part of the reason so many singles feel forced to search out others in an attempt to validate their worth. This has to change.

SINGLE DEFINED

If the media and the world of commerce aren't enough justification for feeling negatively "while unhitched," just the definition of the word *single* as shown in Merriam Webster's

Unabridged Dictionary gives a not-so-good outlook, adding more fear. Let's examine these definitions concerning the word *single*. Be sure to read the commentaries that are included from renowned thinkers from around the globe. They write sentences after the definitions to help the readers understand the context of the word better.

"single"

1 a : living in an unmarried state : CELIBATE *take anything she can get in the way of a husband rather than face penury as a single woman— G.B.Shaw* b : of or relating to celibacy *prefers the single state*

2 : unattended or unaccompanied by others : SOLITARY *he is left alone, single and unsupported, like a leafless trunk— Mirror*

3 a (1) : consisting of or having only one part, feature, or portion as opposed to or contrasted with double or complex *double consonants are often used in place of single consonants* *binocular single vision was tested— H.G.Armstrong* (2) : consisting of one as opposed to or in contrast with many : UNIFORM *undertaking to justify a single scale of rates for the entire country— W.M.W.Splawn* *the states sought a single type of automobile plate* (3) : consisting of only one in number *a single anchor holds the boat* *holds to a single ideal* — often used with not *not a single opponent of statehood appeared before the committee— Midwest Journal* *has not made one single concession to any other quarter— R.T.H.Fletcher* b : having only the normal number of petals or rays : not double — used especially of a horticultural plant *a single rose*

4 a : of or relating to a particular member or part : INDI-
VIDUAL *when nature is so careless of the single life,
why should we coddle ourselves— R.L.Stevenson*
*each single citizen is an important part of the com-
munity* b : of, relating to, or involving only one person
*check his single judgments against a larger concep-
tion or in a perspective of the whole— Meyer Schapiro*
will try his single strength against all the world

5 a obsolete: lacking qualification or addition: PLAIN b
archaic: of poor quality: WEAK *drank his single ale*[1]

Just looking at the definitions of the word *single* will give
you clues as to why singleness is viewed as so potentially negative. Look at the list of negative words on the chart below that
refer to being single. Some of these words come directly from
the definitions and others from the commentary by various
people. Nonetheless, each word is still derived from the whole
concept about being single. I want you to honestly tell me just
how empowered you feel after reading this abridged listing.

Unattended	Unaccompanied	Solitary	Unsupported
Leafless	Lacking	Plain	Poor Quality
Archaic	Left Alone	Weak	Penury

If these words by themselves don't leave a bad taste in
your mouth, just think about the terms that are usually
accompanied by these words.

Unattended. Left alone. Unaccompanied. These
words usually deal with small children and are asso-
ciated with phrases like, "leaving your child alone,"

"putting your child in danger," and the Department of Children and Families, the social organization that will take your children away when you leave them alone. It's against the law!

Solitary. This is a word that most people associate with being imprisoned. You go to solitary confinement, usually as a punishment for doing something horrible, while serving your sentence. They put you in a small confined room that is totally filthy with rats, roaches, and human feces. Can single living really be compared to imprisonment?

Poor quality. It goes with inferior, definitely not the best.

Plain. This word is usually coupled with the name Jane, as in Plain Jane. Calling Jane plain is really a "nicer" way of calling her ugly or homely. Plain is not usually a complimentary word.

Weak. Lacking strength, vulnerable. You are an easy target, defenseless. This word suggests that anyone can do anything that he or she wants to you. Weak people are often taken advantage of.

Archaic. Yet another "non" complimentary word. This word implies that you are totally outdated and irrelevant. You are older than your grandparents and simply not relevant to this modern age.

Lacking. Synonymous words are *poor, impoverished, broke, poverty-stricken, deprived, less fortunate, meager, pitiable, underprivileged, indigent, hard up, on the breadline, bankrupt*, and *penniless*. No further commentary needed.

When condescending words are connected with the word *single*, it's no secret why so many single people think the way they do. The culture overtly sends out messages that you have to have a partner. "You need someone," they'll say. It is conventionally accepted and expected that when a man or woman arrives at a certain age (usually a very young adult age), he or she needs to be concerned with completing his or her perceived "incomplete" life by finding a significant other. To think otherwise will attract immediate opposition.

THE CHURCH'S POSITION

All right, it's one thing for the secular world to have its view on single living. These people don't know God, so their perverted perspectives should be disregarded as quickly as they are being communicated. Believers don't expect any more from them since they've been given a set of false doctrines to believe. I really don't have a major problem with the business sector for its shrewd and sly tactics in trying to reel in fresh and new clientele. Such businesses are doing exactly what they are taught to do: Create a profit. There is nothing intrinsically wrong with that.

In fact, it would be illogical for any sensible businessperson to sit back and refuse to make a sizable profit. Making a huge profit is the primary reason people start businesses. Whether that business markets to single people, married couples, pets, small children, college students, athletes, the hip-hop culture, military personnel, the clergy, or stay-at-home mothers, making a profit is always the underlying objective. So what about the church? Do we too add to the atmosphere of negativity and discomfort that the secular and business worlds impose on single people? The answer to that question, sad to say, is yes.

Like I have already said, we already have low expectations from the worldly to start with. However, it is sad that the church has done equally as much if not more to confuse single people than the world has. Although the Bible makes it very clear what God's view is about single living, both pastors and parishioners continually make singles feel devalued. I'm here to encourage you. I want to let you know that single living is not drudgery and should not be looked on as something malicious. Being single should be your conscious and heartfelt choice—nothing more and nothing less.

Singleness is a choice you make.

You should not be single because no one wants to be with you. If that is your motivation, then you are only being single because you have to be. I've seen more people connect relationally on false pretenses than you could probably imagine. Those kinds of connections rarely if ever are successful. They rarely have any lasting value. For the God-fearing single person who chooses to be single, the decision should be based on the knowledge that he or she can do far more to help advance Christ's kingdom without tending to the earthly and physical needs of a spouse or children. The point that I want to stick with you is that singleness is a choice—and that choice belongs to you.

Although the church is a place where you should receive encouragement from your fellow parishioners, unfortunately it is often more so a place where you feel greatly criticized for taking a stand. That seems quite a bit strange. One would think that the church would uphold and support the values that God prescribed for single living. It would seem that singles within the local church should be celebrated for their conscious desire to commit wholeheartedly to the things of God, rather than be disparaged.

But the enemy seems to have somehow scored again by employing the condemning voices of the saints in an all-out war against singles. Many slurs have been hurled against single Christians that are totally unscriptural and unsubstantiated. After hearing these negative remarks over and over again, one would wonder how single people could withstand such a verbal onslaught. Here are just a few of the main ones that I've heard.

To the single mother with children I've heard said, "You need to get married because your children need a father. You need to have a male role model in the home for your children to follow." As merit worthy as that statement sounds, it's far too late to be making those considerations after the mother has already given birth. That choice should have been made before she decided to sleep with him in the first place. You don't just have children with a man and then pray and wish that the right man would come along to be able to provide and nurture your children. That's backwards.

Or worse yet, you don't waste away your precious life waiting for the man you chose to have children with to make a miraculous change and not be an irresponsible jerk. That doesn't make any sense. Besides, he is not just going to change overnight. Truthfully, he probably won't ever change unless the power of God intervenes. However, that typifies the behavior of many people within our modern common culture. They make bad choices and then try to cover up for them after the mess has settled in.

The proper response from the church should be to encourage the single mother with children to begin to build herself in the Lord through reading the Word of God, actively serving in the church and outreach ministries, and being an example before her children. They should neither force her to marry whosoever comes along, nor make her feel as if she is incomplete not having a man.

Somebody has to stand up as a role model with children to show others that it can be done successfully. I'll talk more about this in Chapter Seven, "Single With Children." But for now, just realize that it is not always God's best for the single mother to marry, especially if the man she is marrying has not been tailor-made to meet her mental, emotional, spiritual, and financial requirements. Added to that, it is far better for her to remain single if she has nothing substantial to offer him either.

Although the single woman gets far more criticism than the single man, the single man is definitely not exempt from the onslaught of venomous slurs either. I've seen young men choosing to serve their pastors as armor bearers, adjutants, and pastoral assistants. Other men who are more artistically driven choose to serve as choir directors, singers, songwriters, and skilled musicians, all of which are greatly needed in the house of the Lord for our worship experiences. However, I've heard young single men and older single men questioned about their sexuality simply because they chose not to get married so they could devote more time to their Christ-like passions.

They have been called derogatory names like faggots, whoremongers, freaks, and womanizers. For the most part this only pushes them further away from the church into the hands of a satanic secular community waiting to welcome them in with open arms. Perhaps that is one of the reasons there are so many young talented men who, though reared in the church, have chosen to follow the hip-hop, rock and roll, and R&B paths once they came of age.

In fact, many of the famous secular musical artists of today (Beyoncé, *American Idol's* Ruben Studdard and Fantasia Barrino, and Brian McKnight) and yesterday (Nat King Cole, Aretha Franklin, Little Richard, and Al Green) got their start in the local church singing gospel music. Put yourself in their shoes if you are not single. Just imagine how single people may feel when they are trying to live for the Lord yet others within their congregation continually make them feel incomplete and unusable because they don't have a spouse.

Singles should not be made to feel like wolves in the local church when their hearts' desire is to be sheep.

I've heard pastors publicly declare that they would rather not have any dealings with the single people in their church; instead, they would prefer to identify with the married couples. They've said, "I would rather spend my time with married couples since they don't pose a threat to my marriage." Just think about how ridiculous that statement actually sounds. Does going out with and spending time with other married couples ensure one's marriage against infidelity? Is it impossible for a married man to have an extramarital affair with a married woman? Of course it isn't. Sin travels in a group as well as alone. Either way, sin is still sin regardless of its packaging.

However, singles are usually the most vulnerable targets of false accusations. They are the ones who are judged most frequently. That's simply unfair. I believe that if a person has a solid marriage then that person doesn't have to shelter him or herself from anybody, whether the other person is single or not. The old adage says, "It takes two to tango." The bottom line is that the strength of a person's marriage is going to be totally predicated on his or her commitments to God and to spouse, not anything else.

When pastors and leaders continue to make single people feel as if they really don't fit into the scope of the vision for the ministry, then there is really no reason for them to continue to linger around. Bluntly put, singles should not have to feel like the wolves in the local church when their hearts' desire is to be a sheep. They should not be viewed as potential threats.

In contradistinction to many churches, the nightclubs in most cities warmly welcome singles. They run promotions and create an environment conducive for singles to feel like they belong. Most believers will agree that the nightclub scene certainly promotes a subtly deceptive negative message. However, they are still far more skilled at attracting singles than the church is because they know how to make them feel worthwhile and connected. If I am single and satisfied, why would I want to attend a ministry where the pastor and the parishioners are constantly reminding me that something is wrong with me because I am not married?

They avoid my presence for fear that I might steal their husband or wife from them. Singles don't have to worry about that kind of drama on the nightclub scene. Everybody there is on an equal playing field. There nobody is all that paranoid about losing anything. God's house needs to be a place where everyone is welcomed, including singles. So the church really is in desperate need of revamping its entire program to make single Christians genuinely feel a part of the whole rather than feel just tolerated.

Another common phrase that you'll hear is, "You're getting old." Most of the time those words are usually directed toward the sisters in the church. "You are 30 years old now, and pretty soon you're not going to be able to have children." They make these women feel as if they need to be in a rush to begin a family. I've heard church mothers encourage young women in their late teens and early twenties to go ahead and get married and start a family. They did not encourage them to go to college and prepare themselves for the real world.

They taught them how to be totally dependent on a man. That mind-set has produced a generation of indolent young women who view men as their "lottery ticket" to personal success and power. The bottom line is that the enemy is the one behind the scenes conjuring up all these false concerns. Today professional women are beginning families later than they traditionally would have started 30 or 40 years ago. Many wise women are choosing to complete their collegiate studies first, so that when they do choose to get married and begin a family they will have a financial base to offer their children.

Far too many babies are born out of wedlock in our country. Too many children are born to "fools for parents" who have not taken into account just how they are going to provide for their child when he or she arrives. Many young people can't afford disposable diapers, infant formula, baby food, baby furniture, clothing, or even decent shelter for their young ones. Yet a confused society looks on them as if they've scored simply for having children. Believe me when I tell you that you have not scored bt having a child. You only score when you make a conscientious effort to provide for that child.

Singleness should be viewed as a wonderful opportunity to sell out for Jesus!

Like week-old bread sitting on the grocer's shelves, the church continually makes singles feel as if they are expiring and their biological faculties are wasting away. Let me warn you, that tactic is only a trick of the enemy to get single women distracted from making a great impact on the kingdom of God. Truthfully, a woman in her 30s or even in her 40s should not be overly worried about whether or not she is able to bear children. God designed a woman's body to be able to bear children. According to the *Guinness World Records 2005,* Special Fiftieth Anniversary Edition, "It was reported that Rosanna dalla Corte {Italy, b February 1931} gave birth to a baby boy on July 18, 1994 when she was 63 years old."[2]

Rosanna dalla Corte is reported to be the oldest mother to give birth to a child, giving birth in her 60s in this modern age, not in Abraham and Sarah's era. That only justifies my point that the enemy uses people within the church to infuse fear into singles' hearts, rendering them useless for kingdom work. The devil always uses fear as his tool of choice to immobilize people. If you are a person who does not live by faith, fear will work against you every time.

If you are a single person in your 30s or 40s, don't worry about it. Don't focus too hard on it. Marriage is a sacred and holy covenant and should never be entered into without knowing for sure that it is a God thing. I did not say a good thing. I said a God thing. When God arranges your marriage, you'll not have to worry about a whole lot of unnecessary drama going on. God knows how to connect the right two people together.

That, however, is something He does in His time, not yours. I've heard church folks say, "You are too good to be by yourself." They ask in a gossiping way, "What's wrong with her? Why isn't she married, as good as she looks? Seems as if everything is going well for her. Why doesn't she have a man?" "Honey, you will make a good wife," or "You are going to make someone a good husband." "If anybody should be married, it should be you; you deserve it."

The list can go on and on seemingly forever. One of the things that often bothered me is that many of these comments usually came from people whose lives were totally screwed up, an absolute mess. Many of the people pushing marriage were not satisfied with their own ruined marriages. They simply wanted other people to feel their pain. You've heard the old adage, "Misery loves company." So for them marriage became a smoke screen, a cover-up. In our society everybody seems far more concerned about appearances than what is actually real. Don't fall into the trap!

Furthermore, most people fail to hail singleness as a glorious opportunity to become a bondservant for Christ. Yes, marriage is honorable and is encouraged in the Scriptures as a vehicle to produce a godly heritage. However, I argue that it is equally as honorable to live a single life totally sold out to Jesus. Neither position is subordinate to the other. Let's consider Paul the apostle's advice to singles in his first letter to the Corinthians. I believe these scriptures provide a solid base for biblical instruction concerning single life.

Although we do not know for sure whether or not Paul was married, it has been widely accepted by theologians that he more than likely was married prior to his conversion. History tells us that Paul was a member of the Sanhedrin. One of the requirements to be a member of the Sanhedrin was that a person had to be married. Many believe that if Paul was married, then his wife most likely died before he converted to Christianity. It was his common sacred practice to forget those things that were in his past. Thus it is very likely that he failed to make mention of his former life, which may have possibly included a wife and children, since they too would have been a part of his prior sinful experiences and consciousness.

Nonetheless, from his writing it is easy to notice that Paul must have had a very close connection and a workable understanding of familial life, making him somewhat of an authority on family structure. Succinctly put, Paul seemed to have known the best of both worlds: singleness and marriage. As a result, he was able to articulately speak to both sides with great value and meaning. Listen to his words.

Now about virgins: I have no command from the Lord, but I give a judgment as one who by the Lord's mercy is trustworthy. Because of the present crisis, I think that it is good for you to remain as you are. Are you married? Do not seek a divorce. Are you unmarried? Do not look for a wife. But if you do marry, you have not sinned; and if a virgin marries, she has not sinned. But those who marry will face many troubles in this life, and I want to spare you this. What I mean, brothers, is that the time is short. From now on those who have wives should live as if they had none; those who mourn, as if they did not; those who are happy, as if they were not; those who buy something, as if it were not theirs to keep; those who use the things of the world, as if not engrossed in them. For this world in its present form is passing away. I would like you to be free from concern. An unmarried man is concerned about the Lord's affairs—how he can please the Lord. But a married man is concerned about the affairs of this world—how he can please his wife—and his interests are divided. An unmarried woman or virgin is concerned about the Lord's affairs: Her aim is to be devoted to the Lord in both body and spirit. But a married woman is concerned about the affairs of this world—how she can please her husband. I am saying this for your own good, not to restrict you, but that you may live in a right way in undivided devotion to the Lord. If anyone thinks he is acting improperly toward the virgin he is engaged to, and if she is getting along in years and he feels he ought to marry, he should do as he wants. He is not sinning. They should get married. But the man who has settled the matter in his own mind, who is under no compulsion but has control over his own will, and who has made up his mind not to marry the virgin—this man also does the right thing. So then, he who marries the virgin does right, but he who does not marry her does even better.

1 Corinthians 7:25-38 NIV

According to this reading, Paul made it clear that the single person can accomplish far more in Christ's kingdom since he or she has no encumbrances. Contextually speaking, the apostle Paul gave his belief on single living based on the age in which he lived. During that time there was not a single moment that the newly established church of the Lord Jesus Christ was not under severe persecution by religious people.

As a result, Christians, by virtue of their profession of faith in Christ, put themselves in a position to be ridiculed, scorned, and possibly tortured to death. Paul felt that it would be unnecessary to subject a potential spouse and small children to such persecution. For that reason he said it would be better for a single person to remain single. Common sense would suggest that it is easier for a person to fend for him or herself than to have to defend his or her entire family.

On the other hand, Paul informed those who were married to stay in their marriages knowing that their commitments to each other honor God. Let's look at a portion of Paul's words again: *"I would like you to be free from concern. An unmarried man is concerned about the Lord's affairs—how he can please the Lord. But a married man is concerned about the affairs of this world—how he can please his wife—and his interests are divided. An unmarried woman or virgin is concerned about the Lord's affairs: Her aim is to be devoted to the Lord in both body and spirit..."* (verses 32-34 NIV).

Paul said a few things here that are applicable both to his era and to this present era in which we live. Please note that when we refer to *unmarried* we are not only referring to men but also to women. So let's infer a few things from this text.

1. I would like you to be free from concern.

Unmarried people have less to worry about than those who are married. Their sole concern is taking care of their own needs, not the needs of others.

2. Unmarried are concerned about the Lord's affairs.

Because the unmarried do not have anyone other than themselves to care for, they are fully available to tend to the affairs of Christ's kingdom.

3. A married man is concerned about the world, about pleasing his wife, and about caring for his family.

God places a high priority on the family. Although God should be first in the life of every believer, God never tries to become the competition of the father, mother, or children in the home. He views them as one unit, the family unit. In the same way that the Father, the Son, and the Holy Spirit are all One God invisible and co-existing, so the family is also.

Married men and women are expected to become great jugglers, tending to the needs of children, spouse, state, church, and society at large. With all these hands in the family, it becomes very difficult for the married person to be as available to God as He would desire for His service.

4. Thus, his interests are divided.

This is not to say that a married woman or man cannot be pleasing to God. Exercising faith is what brings most pleasure to God and both married and unmarried people alike can do that. But a married person will have a very difficult time always being available for Christian service. Singles do not have that problem, which makes them God's choice picks to be used for His glory, unhindered by any other commitments.

The problem is that most single people do not realize that God has need of them. That's why I wrote this book, to prove that you are a needed part of God's plan. Not only does God love you in a singular way, but He also desires to employ your skills, your creativity, and your labor of love to promote His kingdom. Now, we've admitted that secular society has done its part in making singles feel needy. The church has added its share of guilt on singles as well. But you'll have to admit that simply knowing that the God of creation made you for His glory, to fulfill His promises in the earth, is reason enough to begin loving being single all over again. That revelation is just the beginning, however. Let's dig deeper.

ENDNOTES

1. *Merriam Webster's Unabridged Dictionary*, 3.0 (Merriam-Webster Incorporated, 2003), "single."

2. *Guinness World Records 2005*, Special Fiftieth Anniversary Edition (Guinness World Records, Limited, 2004), p. 22.

Chapter Two

BUT I DON'T WANT TO BE ALONE

Autophobia refers to an abnormal and persistent fear of being alone or of oneself.

Monophobia refers to an abnormal and persistent fear of solitude or being alone.

Most people, whether male or female, absolutely hate being alone. That aura has become an ingrained part of American culture. In fact, the few who do choose to be alone are looked on as strange in our society. This mind-set is mostly prevalent within Western thought processes. For example, in India where people practice Hinduism, one is considered to have attained the highest level of spiritual accomplishment at the final stage of life called Sannyasin.

A Sannyasin is a homeless wanderer. He cuts off all ties to his family, changes his name, and divests himself of all possessions except a staff, a begging bowl, and one or two pieces of clothing. He also does not have to follow the religious duties as outlined in their Sacred Law. When interpreting that definition from a Westerner's mind-set, you may at first be inclined to believe that the Sannyasin chooses such a lonely course because he is a former loser who did not attain anything of real value prior to this experience. That is not true.

Large amounts of people who choose this path in Hinduism were former lawyers, medical doctors, university professors, and even *Brahmacarin*, high Hindu priests. Some of these same choosers of the simple paths at one time supported a wife and children, some owned profitable businesses, and many others traveled abroad frequently. So why then would they willingly choose to give up all of their worldly possessions to embrace a lifetime of being alone?

The answer is simple. These precious people have concluded that they can have a greater connection to their god by not having other things or people or possessions to compete for that coveted space. They believe that in order to truly have a connection to their god, they must give total allegiance and attention to him. Any other thing or any other person may have the potential to interrupt the process; thus that person, place, or possession needs to be permanently eliminated in pursuit of what they perceive as peace and true prosperity.

Unfortunately, this is not the view of Westerners. Far worse is the fact that the church of the Lord Jesus Christ has a difficult time relating to this experience. Although the mind-set of leaving all to follow Christ was the ethic and aim of the early disciples, today a new brand of gospel has been forged that declares, "I will follow Jesus if my friends and family can make the trip with me. I will get saved and join the church if my boyfriend or my husband chooses to do the same." The list of "I wills" and "what ifs" can go on and on.

I am merely trying to get you to understand a very simple but yet often overlooked point that many Westerners will follow the tenets of the Christian faith if the others whom we love so dearly choose to do it also. However, if

Even Western Christians so don't want to be alone that they won't follow Christ unless someone else does too.

they do not, then Christ must wait until they are ready before He will receive our total commitment. In the meantime we'll continue to do whatever we can to not appear as being strange, being alone. Many people will go to great measures to avoid being looked at as strange and weird, in this so-called negative image.

I've witnessed mothers and grandmothers being paranoid about living alone and seen the extreme measures they allow in order to have the comfort of knowing someone is there. I've watched them allow their sons and grandsons, daughters and granddaughters live with them as fully grown adult men and women, not contributing anything to the household expenses, utilities, food, and their own personal clothing, yet who are allowed to continue to stay because momma doesn't want to be alone.

I know of situations at this writing where young men are addicted to drugs who steal money and possessions regularly from their mothers to support their addictions, yet who are allowed to continue to live with them. The scenarios do not end at the mother and son relationship. Even married women continue to live in abusive, life-threatening situations where their husbands beat them mercilessly, like the Roman soldiers did to Christ of the cross, yet continue to live in such a repressive environment because they are so afraid of being alone.

Being alone has garnered such a social stigma that just having "someone there" has become many people's primary goal. It really doesn't matter whether or not a man works a job, is faithful to his spouse and family, is abusive or kind, contributes to his wife's overall well-being or constantly tears her down, just as long as he is there. It's all an image thing. There is no real substance; it's all a facade. Even our young people have bought into the hype of the age. You'll hear 12-year-old girls talking about their boyfriends in an effort to assure their listeners that they are normal 12-year-old children—you know, the kind that's not alone.

On top of all that, we come face to face with a scripture in the Bible that if not properly interpreted could easily lead one to believe that God disdained single life. After all, it was God Himself who said that being alone wasn't good. Does God mean what He says and says what He means? I would think so. But it is possible that when God says what He says that the meaning needs to be interpreted in the context in which He said it. It would be meaningless to try and fully understand what He said until we first can grasp why He said what He said. That is what I intend to do.

ALONE OR NOT ALONE?

The LORD God said, "It is not good for the man to be alone. I will make a helper suitable for him."

Genesis 2:18 NIV

Alone or not alone, that is the question at hand. I want to know if being alone is as inherently evil as our society postulates or if being alone has some very redemptive attributes. Can good come out of being by yourself or does one always have to be in the constant companionship of someone in order to experience a genuinely fulfilling life? Some renowned theologians seemed to have a conventional view that celibacy and living without a wife or husband is in error.

According to the well-known *Adam Clarke's Commentary,* Genesis 2:18 seems to support God's opposing viewpoints against being alone. At least that is how Adam Clarke read it. The Bible said: *"It is not good that the man should be alone"* (KJV). Adam Clarke commented these words concerning this verse.

> "As man was made a social creature, it was not proper that he should be alone; for to be alone, i.e. without a matrimonial companion, was not good. Hence, we find that celibacy in general is a thing that is not good, whether it be on the side of the man or of the woman. Men may, in opposition to the declaration of God, call this a state of excellence and a state of perfection; but

let them remember that the word of God says the reverse."[1]

Although Clarke's view on this scripture does not represent every theologian's posture on this issue, it does unfortunately represent widespread majority view concerning this particular text. The semantical problem here is that this verse does not prove God's abhorrence toward the alone lifestyle whatsoever. God declared Himself to be alone, ALL ONE, several times in the Scriptures. It would not make sense for God to command us to be like Him, ALL ONE, while simultaneously condemning the very quality that makes Him unparalleled.

It is God's ability to be alone that creates His mystique, His divine aura, and an air of secrecy. It is this same ability that all people, both married and unmarried alike, strive to achieve in the natural and hope to attain in the spiritual realm by employing some kind of new method. Many married people plan quiet vacations away from the children, away from their co-workers, and far from their schoolmates, all in a conscious attempt to find aloneness.

In some ways it seems like a fiscal trap. On one hand there are the businesses that make single people feel absolutely rotten about their lives. They market creative ways to get singles to buy into the ideology of hooking up with someone. Then on the other hand you have married people and couples who become the prime targets of private getaways, personal relaxation, spas, and body treatment facilities.

Clarke made some strong unbalanced statements that have become commonly accepted as truth but simply do not weigh strongly in light of God's Word. For example, statements such as, "It was not proper that he should be alone" and "without a matrimonial companion, was not good" and "we find that celibacy in general is a thing that is not good, whether it be on the side of the man or of the woman. Men may, in opposition to the declaration of God, call this [celibate living] a state of excellence and a state of perfection; but let them remember that the word of God says the reverse."

The reason I chose this commentator's words is because his seem to be the compendium of all the others I've read. His comments lead one to believe that everybody's destiny is marriage. Although the Word of God tells us to flee from fornication, Clarke tells us that celibacy in general terms is not a good thing. The apostle Paul called celibacy a gift; God considers it a grace; yet Clarke says that celibacy is in opposition to God's Word. Now I am not sure about you, but that is quite confusing to me.

How can celibacy be wrong? God could not have meant for all people on earth to be married in order for His sovereign approval to be placed upon them. If that were the case, then God would not have allowed a celibate man such as Paul to write nearly two-thirds of the New Testament. Man's redemption would somehow be tied into his or her ability to find a sufficient mate rather than receiving the finished work of Jesus. So if God was not condemning single living, why then did He say in Adam's hearing that it was not good for man to be alone?

"Being alone" did not mean what most people think it means. It did not mean not having someone to spend time with, although that is very important and has great value and meaning. It did not mean not having a wife. If having a wife were good in every context, then every man who found a wife would receive God's favor. *"He who finds a wife finds a good thing, and obtains favor from the LORD"* (Proverbs 18:22).

Interestingly, when you look at the many married people you know, they don't appear to have God's favor. Some do, yet many do not. It's quite possible that

"Being alone" did not mean what most people think it means.

God is saying that in order to find a wife, you will need My favor. You've heard the saying before, "A good woman is hard to find." And in order to find a rare jewel such as a "good woman," you'll need much more than good looks, a college degree, and glib lines. You will need God's power. And His power is the one thing that nearly everyone who seeks out a spouse forgets to access.

I will make a helper suitable for him.

Genesis 2:18b NIV

Being alone is not good in direct connection to the lack of help needed to fulfill one's purposes in God. For example, God's Word says, *"And God blessed them, saying, 'Be fruitful and multiply, and fill the waters in the seas, and let birds multiply on the earth' "* (Genesis 1:22). This mandate to be fruitful and multiply could never happen without the help, the assistance, and the coming together of man and woman. Although this scripture can be looked at from a sexual point of view, it has to be viewed far beyond that in order to receive its deepest revelation.

God is establishing in this scripture the value and the basis for interdependence. He is suggesting that nothing of value will ever be birthed if men continue to think they can birth things alone. Naturally this is impossible. God is saying it is not good for man to be alone because when he is alone he has the tendency to believe that he can multiply by himself. He believes that he can produce good on his own. He falsely believes that he does not need God for his sustenance. Again, you must consider the context of this verse. This was written in an era where society was predominantly patriarchal. Men were the dominating class.

It is not good to be alone in connection to the need for help in fulfilling one's purposes in God.

In this egotistical era, women were not considered valuable. To continue the lineage of a man's posterity, male babies were preferred to female babies. The problem with this patriarchal mind-set is that God told both man and woman to have dominion over the earth, not one alone. If dual dominion would ever take place, male men would have to recognize that standing as governors, rulers, and progenitors would have to be a shared responsibility and that they could no longer consider it good to do those things alone.

How could being alone (meaning without a spouse) be inherently evil when Jesus lived a fulfilled and successful life without a spouse? What Jesus recognized and what so many people fail to realize is that women such as Mary and Martha played integral roles in the plan for His life. Even the women who waited at the tomb to see whether He would be raised up on the third day or not were a part of His purpose. Although they were not married to Jesus in the literal sense, they still refused to leave Him alone. It not would have been good to leave Him alone.

Some may deny it, but the real truth is that every human being on this earth truly desires to be alone. It is only in this stance that a person can really discover who he or she really is. More than that, we can only truly experience God in an ultimate sense when we are alone. This train of belief is substantiated all throughout the Scriptures by studying out the lives of various people in pursuit of God. When they came to the point of serious pursuit, they knew intuitively that they could not carry any family or friends with them for this ride. They could only experience God most intimately, alone.

JACOB WAS LEFT ALONE—A GOOD THING

So Jacob was left alone, and a man wrestled with him till daybreak. When the man saw that he could not overpower him, he touched the socket of Jacob's hip so that his hip was wrenched as he wrestled with the man. Then the man said, "Let me go, for it is daybreak." But Jacob replied, "I will not let you go unless you bless me." The man asked him, "What is your name?" "Jacob," he answered. Then the man said, "Your name will no longer be Jacob, but Israel, because you have struggled with God and with men and have overcome."

Genesis 32:24-28 NIV

Jacob received the greatest blessing of his lifetime when he wrestled with the angel of the Lord alone. A former con artist and master swindler, Jacob realized that his previous lifestyle of dishonesty and double-crossing family members could not last. He realized that he needed a totally new identity. His past reputation had been so marred that it would inevitably spoil any chances of him having a promising future. Realizing that, Jacob became infuriated with his present self.

He became so desperate for a name change that he continued to grapple with the angel even to the point of displacing his own hip. Because of his doggedness and obvious sincerity, God granted him his desire, a new identity. His name was changed from Jacob to Israel. Not only were Israel and his descendants God's chosen people, but also from his loins would emerge one of the greatest nations in the world.

This major transference of spiritual endowment could have never been made possible had Jacob decided to receive his blessing in the company of others. Jacob came to realize a profound truth that every single person should adopt as his or her creed—God gives His best blessings not in the midst of the masses but in solitary confinement. It is in these lonely places that He is able to perform His greatest work on the soul of man, away from the many distractions that life offers.

MOSES WAS LEFT ALONE

And the Angel of the LORD appeared to him in a flame of fire from the midst of a bush. So he looked, and behold, the bush was burning with fire, but the bush was not consumed. Then Moses said, "I will now turn aside and see this great sight, why the bush does not burn." So when the LORD saw that he turned aside to look, God called to him from the midst of the bush and said, "Moses, Moses!" And he said, "Here I am." Then He said, "Do not draw near this place. Take your sandals off your feet, for the place where you stand is holy ground."

Exodus 3:2-5

Moses would have never seen himself as the great deliverer that he actually was until he was alone with the Lord. You see, although we do not realize it, we become like the people we choose to be around most often. And it is those people who brand our image with their impression. Moses spent 40 years on the backside of the desert, without title or status, just alone. It was in this place that he became comfortable with himself, but more than that, comfortable with his God.

Without even realizing it Moses became intimately connected to God so much so that God was able to speak to Moses of a new vocation. At first Moses would refuse to accept the job offer. Moses could have easily reminded himself that he was just the opposite of a deliverer, having killed an innocent man some years prior. Had he been in the company of any of his accusers or witnesses, they would have surely reminded him of what he did, forcing him to see himself as a victim of his past.

When God appeared to Moses at the bush, it was far more than just another ethereal experience. God was making a bold statement. He was conveying the message that your life is not the sum total of what you have done in your past, but rather what you are doing right now. Despite what you may have done before, the blood of the Lamb can redeem you if you allow God to redirect your life. Imagine the headline: FORMER MURDERER BECOMES DELIVERER OF A NATION. In our modern culture, that would have surely made the front page of *The New York Times*. Such a great transformation not only was designed for Moses but also is available for you. Amazing things happen when you willingly walk with God—with or without other folks.

JOHN THE REVELATOR WAS LEFT ALONE

I, John, both your brother and companion in the tribulation and kingdom and patience of Jesus Christ, was on the island that is called Patmos for the word of God and for the testimony of Jesus Christ. I was in the Spirit on the Lord's Day, and I heard behind me a loud voice, as of a trumpet, saying, "I am the Alpha and the Omega, the First and the Last," and, "What you see, write in a book and send it to the seven churches which are in Asia: to Ephesus, to Smyrna, to Pergamos, to Thyatira, to Sardis, to Philadelphia, and to Laodicea."

Revelation 1:9-11

Being a writer, I can clearly identify with John's position. There are times when I really need to get away from the rigorous routine of preaching, teaching, and motivating people around the world simply to find time enough to hear from God. Some consider John's exile to the small island of Patmos as a type of imprisonment or punishment. Just knowing John's character, I would venture to say that John viewed his sentencing as a blessing in disguise.

As occupied and full as John's life actually was, this one time John could clearly hear the voice of the Lord for the churches in Asia. The Word of God to these churches was perhaps the most relevant Word and for some the most relevant warning that they would ever hear. Had John not been alone on this island or had he been distracted by mundane pursuits, he would have sadly missed the voice of the Lord and the seven churches in Asia would not have been duly warned of the impeding sentence that God was imposing on them unless they changed their ways.

John's time alone literally saved the church. Imagine how many lives, institutions, and families could actually be changed if you chose to be alone for the purpose of spending quality time with God? I would even venture to say that there may be a writing genius inside of you. You may have the gift to write songs, movies, plays, and music scores.

The only problem is that your life is so cluttered with everyone else's concerns that you can't hear anything from within to write down. There may very well be great inventions waiting to be discovered living inside of you. You may have the cure for AIDS, but have not yet set aside the necessary time to cultivate the soil that will produce your own hidden genius.

Maybe you too need to find a secluded island where you can find peace and quietness away from life's apparent and subtle distractions and diversions. No wonder so many writers choose secluded areas of the world to write their most prized works. God is writing His words on the thin lining of your soul. You need no interpreter to construe its meaning. All you need is time alone.

JESUS WAS LEFT ALONE

Then they came to a place which was named Gethsemane; and He said to His disciples, "Sit here while I pray." And He took Peter, James, and John with Him, and He began to be troubled and deeply distressed. Then He said to them, "My soul is exceedingly sorrowful, even to death. Stay here and watch." He went a little farther, and fell on the ground, and prayed that if it were possible, the hour might pass from Him. And He said, "Abba, Father, all things are possible for You. Take this cup away from Me; nevertheless, not what I will, but what You will."

Mark 14:32-36

Of course I would be remiss if I did not mention the very One Himself, Jesus Christ, the personification of excellence in single living. During what I would classify as the greatest challenge of His life, Jesus faced the inevitable gloom of having to endure the shame and pain of the crucifixion alone. His alone experience started out in Gethsemane, with three of His disciples, Peter, James, and John. Although these three disciples were the closest to the heart of Christ, even they could not comfort their Lord but for a short point in time.

When faced with the reality of what was to come, Jesus had to deal with His Father alone. There is no one Jesus loved as much as He loved His Father, and being separated from the Father even for a moment was tantamount to the most lethal death. Yet He had to endure this great suffering alone. It would seem fair by most human standards that Jesus should have had the help, counsel, and consoling of His most faithful disciple and followers. Surely Mary and Martha would have willingly and proudly bore the beatings and the punishment on behalf of their Savior.

Had it been possible for Jesus to apportion a small part of His necessary chastisement to His followers, then He would not have had to deal with as much pressure as He withstood. Jesus again reminds all of us that some things in life we have to do on our own, particularly those things that are directly connected to a promise. One thing is for sure, and that is this: If you go through your process alone, no one can share the spoils of your victory with you when God elevates you. In the final analysis, your alone time will always be worth the while.

> *Therefore God also has highly exalted Him and given Him the name which is above every name, that at the name of Jesus every knee should bow, of those in heaven, and of those on earth, and of those under the earth, and that every tongue should confess that Jesus Christ is Lord, to the glory of God the Father.*
>
> Philippians 2:9-11

I DON'T NEED YOUR APPROVAL— I'VE ALREADY BEEN APPROVED

When you receive the revelation that God has already approved and sanctioned who you are, you will no longer seek out the approval of man in life. So many singles do too much to try to gain the approval of the people they have an interest in. The only problem is, once you have bought into the cycle of trying to get approved, you wind up making thousands of concessions and still never make them happy. Worse yet, *you* are not happy when all is said and done and the changes have been complete. For example, you're a little chubby and in order to get approved you wind up going on the Hollywood diet. It lasted a few days but it is over in no time. Your commitment dies.

The real truth is that your success is directly correlated to your ability to DO IT ALONE, regardless of what popular society thinks or suggests. The late Ester Schaler Bucholz, Ph.D., professor of applied psychology at New York University School of Education and author of *The Call of Solitude: Alonetime in a World of Attachment,* writes: "Along with language barriers, societal de-mands instill fear of going it alone. Why does society ardently decry alonetime? Could it be that the lure to be alone is so great that strong counter-measures are always employed?"[2]

> *Your success is directly correlated to your ability to do it alone.*

I believe that it is very possible that the negative powers that be realize how important being alone is and how central it is to our overall development and progress. These powers also recognize how valuable you will actually become if you spend time alone, how appreciating your worth will actually become, and how that will inevitably improve the declining condition of humanity. You can only change the world when you have had time to develop your innermost self.

I'll leave this chapter with Bucholz's words:

The quiet containment in the stretch of time before birth hardly prepares us for the dependent helpless-ness immediately after. Seeds may be planted within that state of helplessness—the seeds of fear—and if they are allowed to blossom and spread, they could well interfere with a wonderful inner garden of alone life experiences. Those fears, together with social preconceptions and today's myopic focus on bonding needs, keep hidden a vital awareness of the need for alone-time.[3]

"Great minds that perform great feats are birthed in lonely soil yet harvested by the masses." –Unknown

For God has not given us a spirit of fear, but of power and of love and of a sound mind.

2 Timothy 1:7

ENDNOTES

1. *Adam Clarke's Commentary*, Electronic Database. Copyright © 1996 by Biblesoft.

2. Ester Schaler Bucholz, *The Call of Solitude: Alonetime in a World of Attachment* (Simon & Schuster, 1997), p. 31.

3. Bucholz, *The Call of Solitude*, p. 27.

Chapter Three

UNDERSTANDING THE BEAUTY OF SINGLENESS

———⟶⟩●⟨⟵———

Being single is a beautiful thing. I realize that you have not always heard it or perceived it that way, but it's really true. We've already covered the world's perspective on your single state of being. But I would be remiss if I failed to inform you of God's view about singleness. God articulately declares His passionate feelings about you in His Word. He does not describe you coupled with someone else. He deals with each individual in His creation one by one.

Like a master artist, God has made you the most unique one in His creative portfolio. There is no one else quite like you in this world. One of God's major objectives is to convey that message to you. And He is willing to go to great lengths to communicate that message to you. It is one thing to hear it being said or even read, but it is far more effective when you believe what you hear and have accepted it as the whole truth. That truth is, you are beautiful just the way you are. With or without someone else, you are singularly dazzling. God knows it; now you need to know it as well.

YOU ARE FEARFULLY AND WONDERFULLY MADE

I will praise You, for I am fearfully and wonderfully made; marvelous are Your works, and that my soul knows very well. My frame was not hidden from You, when I was made in secret, and skillfully wrought in the lowest parts of the earth. Your eyes saw my substance, being yet unformed. And in Your book they all were written, the days fashioned for me, when as yet there were none of them.

Psalm 139:14-16

Just think about the consistency of the human structure. Yet it is vastly complex in every way. How can a bone that begins in the life of an embryo so small and fragile continue to grow and develop all the way through adulthood? Why doesn't the human heart just stop to take a break from all of its continuous beating? Anything that is driven continuously will eventually break down. You can't drive a car non-stop or fly a plane without getting it serviced periodically. But the human heart was designed to continue pumping and moving blood through the veins.

Your body was designed to heal itself. Few can argue that you were wonderfully made. But you are also fearfully made. You were designed ever so exquisitely nice and fragile that the slightest mishap may damage or possibly destroy in a moment's time some of your body parts that are necessary for your survival. So in making you God has done two all-important things. One thing He has done is shown you how phe-nomenal your intricate inner workings are. He showed you that, given the right circum-stances and care, your body can live a very long time.

You are both tough and fragile at the same time.

On the other hand, if you should disrespect the body that He gave you, you may easily die from your negligence. You are both tough and fragile at the same time. He made you tough and enduring to remind you of the quality of eternity that both you and He have in common. God made you frag-ile and weak to give you a constant reminder of His divine providence and your lifelong dependency on Him.

"Fearfully" in this scripture is the Hebrew word *yare* (Strong's #H3372). It has to do with the concept of God's infi-nite power being the impetus to inspire reverence toward Him. Yet another way of looking at this translation is "I am fearfully separated." Every God-fearing believer has been separated and made distinguishably different than the ungod-ly. The Spirit of God designed you and you are now separat-ed from all the people who are yet lost within the old Adam.

In some ways it is like a microchip built on the inside of you that will always remind you to tremble at the awesome-ness of God while simultaneously adoring everything about Him. Only you have this feature. Animals, fish, and insects do not have this level of consciousness. Although the plant king-dom recognizes the presence of God, they cannot respond back in the way that you and I can. You are made like no one else in the world. Before anyone saw any value in you, God first saw great value in you. Knowing that alone should make all the difference in the world to you.

That is why God hid you in His workshop for so long. You were made in secret, but not by the hands of a novice. No, the Master's hands skillfully worked on you. That is the main reason you are so sensitive to ill treatment. That is why you get all bent out of shape when you are not loved like you think you should be, caressed often, and treated with the utmost respect. You were first touched by God's hands, so no one else's hands will ever feel quite the same in your search unless they know God personally and treat you with the same level of care that He would.

YOU ARE MADE IN THE IMAGE OF GOD

Then God said, "Let Us make man in Our image, according to Our likeness; let them have dominion over the fish of the sea, over the birds of the air, and over the cattle, over all the earth and over every creeping thing that creeps on the earth." So God created man in His own image; in the image of God He created him; male and female He created them

Genesis 1:26-27

You are made in the image of the all mighty, all-encompassing, incomparable Holy God. Both now and at the time of your beginning God viewed you as a very substantial part of His creation. So much so that He chose to create you in His own image after His own likeness. He could have chosen to fashion you after so many different kinds of species. But because you were so special to Him, He reserved the right to fashion you after Himself, leaving nothing to chance.

What does all that mean? It simply means that you are like God in every way. Your beauty, your elegance, your ability to make rational choices, your character, and your desire to win all reflect the image of your Creator. When you look into the mirror, what do you see? Do you see a complexion that *Only God can tell you how much you are worth.* is dark, light, pale, or tanned? Do you see yourself with long hair, a short hairdo, a winning smile, a depressive frown, or a pile of bones and flesh laden with low-self esteem?

If you do see any of those things, you are looking into the mirror of your subconscious reality, which more often than not is an illusion. You have heard so many negative affirmations throughout the course of your entire life that it has now somewhat affected your psyche. It is impossible for your worth to ever be determined by a freelance appraiser. Only God can tell you how much you are worth. After all, He is the manufacturer.

It would be quite senseless for the Hyundai Corporation to try to determine or set the price on a new or used Lexus. In order for them to find out the worth of the vehicle, they would inevitably have to go back to the maker to get an idea of the value. At best they'll only still be able to make a close guess. You are far greater than a Lexus, Mercedes Benz, or Bentley Continental, yet you've allowed people to diminish your image time and time again because you forgot in whose image you were made.

There is another fine point that I would like to make about the image of God. The very first time that God's name was mentioned in the Bible, it introduced His name as Jehovah Elohim, the God who was busy creating. Don't miss this point! From the very beginning of time, God has been creating things and has never stopped until this very moment. You are created in His image, so that means you too should be creating things of lasting worth all the time.

There are businesses inside of you, ministries that have yet to be birthed, and legacies to be built. Inside of you are songs, visions, dreams, books, patents, and inventions all lying dormant. The very nature of God's image is to create. Creating should also be a natural part of who you are. Perhaps you haven't been creating because you were waiting for someone else to create with you.

Maybe you were afraid to build because your subconscious mind told you that you could not build without the help of the masses. Here's the truth: Once you begin, once you initiate the process of creating, God will bring all the necessary help, resources, finances, and opportunities you need to get the job done. The bottom line is that you've got to start somewhere. Why not now?

Not only are you God's express image with creative proclivities, you also are made to have dominion. Don't be mistaken; God did not create you to dominate other people. That will always end up in a quarrel. You women were not made to dominate a man, and a man was not made to dominate a woman. Wives are not supposed to dominate their husbands and neither should husbands control their wives.

Only God has the authority and express privilege of dominating humans. He is the only One who can be trusted with such a great responsibility. Any time another human takes on this position, it will always end up being far out of God's will. That is when people get into human subjugation and slavery. God has called us to have dominion over non-human entities. He lists these entities in Genesis: *"over the fish of the sea, over the birds of the air, and over the cattle, over all the earth and over every creeping thing that creeps on the earth."*

We should rule over the animal kingdom. That's why so many children ask for pets when they are small. "Mommy, Daddy, can you buy me a dog, or a cat, a gerbil, a guinea pig, a rattlesnake, a ferret?" I'm sure you get the point. Children are born with a built-in desire to have dominion over something. More than that, God called you to take dominion over evil forces that can impede your spiritual progress. We have power over demons and anything that exalts itself against the knowledge of God.

There is really no middle ground. Either we take control over the devil or he will take control over us. Being created in the image of God means that when the devil sees you he should be sore afraid, realizing that you have the same power to destroy his works just like God does. The image of God equips you to be the most positive, strong, and coura-geous single you can be. In fact, it is the most powerful knowledge that any believer can ever be armed with. That is why the enemy fights so hard to try to get you to believe otherwise. You are a powerful somebody!

I have given you authority to trample on snakes and scorpions and to overcome all the power of the enemy; nothing will harm you.

Luke 10:19 NIV

YOU ARE HANDMADE

Your hands have made me and fashioned me; give me understanding, that I may learn Your commandments.

Psalm 119:73

I've always been a connoisseur of fine things. For example, I really love Patek Phillipe watches. Patek watches are handmade in Switzerland by a master watchmaker and each one takes at least nine months to complete. The inner workings of each watch are intricately detailed. The timing on each watch is perfectly set. The outer watch is usually laid with 18 karat gold filling. Some special editions also may include fine diamonds around the face of the watch. It may come with an alligator wristband, a leather band, or an 18 karat gold band to match the watch. Each watch comes with a lifetime warranty. The average cost of such a fine piece of work is usually between $15,000 and $30,000.

Why would anyone even care to have a watch so costly and rare? Let's face it; you could buy a Timex watch for $40 or $50 anywhere. The Timex will more than likely work and tell accurate time just like the Patek. So why invest so much? The reason most people buy a Patek watch is not so much with themselves in mind but rather the generation after them. Each piece becomes an heirloom. It is passed down from generation to generation. In the same way God expects that His investment in you will be passed down to successive generations.

An Omas Celluloid pen or a Montegrappa Extra 1912 pen is valued at about $1,000 each and takes about 360 days to make. Again, you could buy a ten pack of Bic pens for about

$3.99 from Staples or Office Max, making each pen about 39 cents. Each pen will write the same. Both the Bic pen and the Omas or Montegrappa will communicate the same message on a piece of paper. Why bother paying so much for a simple pen? You must realize that you are not merely buying a pen, but rather a work of fine art. You are purchasing a small piece of someone's life and energy and ingenuity.

Whether a pen, a timepiece, an Italian leather living room set, a rare painting, or an Aston Martin car, things that are handmade will always take longer to make and will retain their value in years to come. In this same manner you are not a carbon copy. God did not scan you from a high tech Hewlett Packard scanner. It wasn't such a simple process. God made you by hand. He knew that anything that He made with His hands would continue to appreciate over time.

God expects that His investment in you will be passed down to successive generations.

Unfortunately, we often associate with people who may not recognize how much we are really worth and who may tend to devalue us. What you must recognize is that God's creations never lose their value, even if they show up in the wrong places from time to time. An A quality diamond is worth no less in the flea market than it is in the pig's pen or at Tiffany's.

The diamond is still the diamond no matter where it is. Once you recognize the diamond on the inside of you, you will begin to start associating yourself only with people who value your truest worth. You won't bother hanging around with people who try to cheapen you and put you down. Rather, you will only connect with people who have an ability to sharpen you and make you better. Handmade items are never in abundance, but they are always rare.

Handmade objects had a whole lot of work go into their development process, which makes them come off of the assembly line with a very high price. No wonder you came from God's private workshop with such a high cost—you are handmade. No matter what has happened in your past or what may happen in the future, nothing in the world will ever change the fact that you have been crafted by the most powerful and influential hands in the universe: God's hands.

The precious sons of Zion, valuable as fine gold, how they are regarded as clay pots, the work of the hands of the potter!

Lamentations 4:2

As you do not know what is the way of the wind, or how the bones grow in the womb of her who is with child, so you do not know the works of God who makes everything.

Ecclesiastes 11:5

Chapter Four

EVANGELISTIC DATING

DECEPTIVE DATING

Let's talk about the deceptions of dating people who are unsaved. This is an area of grave danger. The reason this area is so unsafe is because it is the sole area the enemy uses to infiltrate God's holy church with his malicious brand of worldly corruption. What I mean by that is, the majority of sin that creeps into the church does not get in through the doors by force. Usually it comes in through private invitation.

Once sin arrives it is warmly welcomed by the fellow parishioners. After a while the unsaved and their sins feel so at home that they decide to make the church a permanent dwelling place, receiving all the rights and privileges of the fellow parishioners. Once they have made the church their resting place, they begin to set up shop in the temple, inviting in every conceivable iniquity within. When we know this information, we must guard the gates of the temple with all diligence. Otherwise our churches will be ruined.

I've kind of summarized the source of the problem, but I did not elaborate on how this problem actually breeds itself. How does it all happen? Where does it all start? Where is that entry point? It all starts with a phrase that I have coined: "evangelistic dating." What exactly is evangelistic dating? Let's first look at what dating is. Dating, simply put, is being in a romantic relationship with a person. Interestingly, dating does not imply simply being in a relationship with another person. It specifically has to include romance to distinguish it from any other type of relationship.

For example, sharing a friendship with someone is just as much a relationship as two people who date. A friendship is a relationship in which two people relate through being friends. On this level there can be a very spiritual and soul intimacy taking place, even though they both remain in a totally platonic state. However, romance (which is directly correlated to dating), by the very definition of the word, implies a sense of fantasy or that which is not real. Look at the definition of romance.

"romance"

1 : consisting of or similar in form or content to a romance *romantic fiction*

2 : having no basis in fact: being the product of invention or exaggeration: FABULOUS, IMAGINARY *liked to make observations all his own and give his characteristic romantic report afterward*

3 : impractical in conception or plan: UNREALISTIC, VISIONARY *some romantic get-rich-quick scheme to attain a heaven-on-earth*[1]

You can clearly see words attached to its meaning such as *fiction, no basis, exaggeration, fabulous, imaginary, impractical,* and *unrealistic.* After reading that list, I wonder if anyone could honestly say that dating in the sense that we have come to understand it in the Western world is of any value at all. If you have ever dated before or if you have ever known a person who dated, you should be able to easily recognize some if not all of these characteristics in the relationship.

Isn't it true that most women dream of having a man come and sweep them off of their feet—you know, the Prince Charming type or should I say the Denzel Washington or Brad Pitt type? They dream about the big white colonial house way out in the suburbs sitting on two acres, with a pool in the backyard, a two-car garage, the Mercedes Benz wagon, a 7 series BMW, two kids, and a golden retriever. That sounds like fiction to me. I am not suggesting that this scenario is impossible; I am merely stating that without the proper groundwork set in place that dream will never become a reality.

Worse yet are the women and men who frequent bars and nightclubs in expectation of finding a quality lifelong partner. That train of thought is outright impractical and unrealistic. In most bars and nightclubs you'll find the same kinds of people: those looking for love and usually willing to go to any lengths to receive it. Unfortunately, most of the clubbers don't know what true love is, so for the most part hot and sizzling cheap sex usually suffices for the moment.

In general the faithful clubbers possess an unusual amount of low self-esteem. Many are just looking to be affirmed, recognized, and wanted by someone. Sad to say, they just don't realize that the club scene has to be the absolute worst place on earth to find valuable long-lasting relationships. I wouldn't lie to you. You can find a one-night stand if that is what you are looking for, but nothing more than that. So for the most part avoid the nightclub scene because it is a great deception that far too many gullible people buy into.

Have you ever been lied to by a person who wanted to date you? Has anyone over-exaggerated claims about him or herself just to impress you? Personally, I think that I must have heard it all or at least been close to having heard it all. I have heard men lie to women about owning brand-new cars such as Mercedes Benzs, BMWs, Bentleys, Jaguars, Lexuses, and Porsches, while not even owning a car at all. I mean they didn't even own a bucket.

These men went out on dates in their girlfriend's car by night and walked everywhere else they went by day. They've said, "I own a five-bedroom house with a three-car garage." The real truth was that they lived in the basement of their mom's house. "I work on the sixtieth floor of the Gold Building, and I earn $100,000 annually." The truth of the matter is that the Gold Building does not have a sixtieth floor; the highest floor is the fourteenth. And about the $100,000 annual income—he really does not have a job at all.

How about college degrees? I've met more Ph.D.'s that haven't even earned an associate degree. They've claimed to have attended Yale, Harvard, Stanford, Princeton, Oxford, Brown, and MIT. They don't even have a GED. I can't help but also mention that they have "traveled all over the world touring and studying." If the truth were told, they've never been past the city limits of the city they were born in.

I believe that the greatest lie of them all is when married men swear that they are not married or never have been married even though their wife and children are waiting patiently at home for them. Why the lies? Why all the exaggeration and hyperbole? It is all a part of the conventional dating scene. It's all a part of the deep deception of dating.

When people date, the truth is rarely revealed.

When people date, the truth is rarely revealed. After all, you want the other person to know only the things about you that are merit worthy. Every negative thing about yourself remains hidden, tucked away in a secret place while dating. I mean, you're not really supposed to tell the truth to the people you are trying to impress. Or are you? If they knew the real you, if they could discover the person hiding beneath the surface of the façade, then they might not want to be with you anymore.

What if she really knew that you hated your mother? Would she still trust you? How about if he knew that you were just released from the mental institution? Did you tell him that you worship Satan from time to time? Or did you confess that from time to time you are pretty confused about your sexual identity? How about the time you got arrested for going on a six-store stealing binge—did you tell him all about that?

Did you tell the other person that you were a compulsive liar, were a thief, were a child molester, had horrible credit, could not be trusted, lived a double life, had split personalities, had an uncontrollable temper, were physically and verbally abusive, and were downright undependable? Of course not! If

You will not win a person to Jesus because you compromise your faith.

you told your date all those things, you would scare him or her away. After all, the truth does make one free, but which one? In dating we put on our happy face to cover the wrinkles from our permanent frown.

So what is evangelistic dating? Evangelistic dating is not much different than conventional dating. In fact, they are very much alike. Both have all the built-in deceptions, except one

far more deadly ingredient is added to the list for evangelistic dating. The whole idea behind evangelism is that you are intentionally trying to use every tool and method possible to get someone to receive the Lord Jesus Christ. Well, some Christian people tend to believe that if they date sinners long enough, those sinners will eventually become converts. They use dating pagans as a way to get people connected to God.

Nothing could be further from reality. You will not win a person to Jesus because you compromise your faith. In fact, the person with whom you compromise your faith will be the more unlikely person to ever receive Christ, seeing that your sloppy witness further discouraged him or her. You can't have sex with a sinner on Saturday night and then invite your partner to church on Sunday morning hoping and praying that he or she will respond to the invitation for salvation. It does not work like that.

I have never seen a Christian date a sinner and God bless that union. It has never happened. For the most part the

Christian usually becomes so weakened by the association that he or she begins to decline spiritually at a rapid pace. You can't win sinners by doing the same sins that they do, especially with them. To believe otherwise is only grossly deceiving to both parties.

ARE YOU A VIRTUOUS PERSON OR A DEPRECIATING ASSET?

What are you worth? That is a question that you will have to answer at some point in your life. You cannot expect to live a quality single life until you are first able to answer this question in the affirmative with great conviction. The bottom line is that people will always be inclined to treat you like you treat yourself. You set the stage. You give them the example in yourself to follow.

I've heard so many sisters say, "There aren't any good men in the church. And the ones who are there are all married." That untrue statement has been the main reason so many young women have sought out unsaved men as a viable alternative. The enemy has convinced you of a lie. Believe me when I tell you that there are literally millions of qualified, handsome, financially secure, and "loving the Lord with all their heart" single men out there. In fact, they are all around, just waiting to notice you.

You ask, "Then why can't I find any of these men? They must be in hiding." The answer is quite simple. You cannot still have the remnant of the same spirit on you that you had when you were in the world and expect to attract a godly man. That world-like aura has not left you. Once it does leave, believe me when I tell you that you will not be attracting people who are not born again. I believe with all my heart that in life you will always attract who you are.

Both men and women have mastered the art of telling each other what the other would like to hear. They know how to say all the right things. They don't mind you serving God in the beginning because they are trying to win you. They don't want to do anything stupid to scare you away. They don't mind your going to church, particularly if you don't make any demands on them to attend church with you. They'll do everything in the beginning to put on a happy face.

People will always be inclined to treat you like you treat yourself.

They'll come to the church outings, all the free functions, and of course the dinners. But when it comes to making a heartfelt commitment to the Lord and His church, that's when you will discover the devil that he really is. The only problem is that by that time it's far too late and the damage has already been done to your life—damage that may take months and even years to undo. So the solution is simple. Beware of the unbeliever as it relates to dating and you will be safer.

You say, "I've dated saved men who acted just as devilish as the sinner did. What about that?" The bottom line is that if both so-called saved men and unsaved men are acting like outright sinners toward you, it's obvious that there is something on you or in you that needs to be sanctified. Now I'm not here to bring condemnation on you or to cast judgment on anybody. Judgment belongs to the Lord. However, I do know that if I tried to bleach a stain out of my shirt and it still remained after one washing, I may need to wash it over again until the stain is totally gone.

The blood of Jesus that washes away sin also can wash away the negative aura that you carried while you were in sin. When Jesus has truly washed away the stain off your life, you begin to appreciate in value. The funny thing is that everyone around you notices just how much you went up in value. The guys from your past will look at you and suddenly see the glory of the Lord over you.

They will know instinctively that you are not cheap, that your price is far above rubies. Most of all, they will know that they can no longer afford you because you have been purchased for a high price, a price far above any amount of money. They'll know that you have been bought by the sacrificial death of Christ and nothing in the world they could do will ever match that. As a result you will no longer attract them. Better yet, they won't be attracted to you.

SOLOMON'S GREAT FOLLY

But King Solomon loved many foreign women, as well as the daughter of Pharaoh: women of the Moabites, Ammonites, Edomites, Sidonians, and Hittites—from the nations of whom the LORD had said to the children of Israel, "You shall not intermarry with them, nor they with you. Surely they will turn away your hearts after their gods." Solomon clung to these in love. And he had seven hundred wives, princesses, and three hundred concubines; and his wives turned away his heart. For it was so, when Solomon was old, that his wives turned his heart after other gods; and his heart was not loyal to the LORD his God, as was the heart of his father David. For Solomon went after Ashtoreth the goddess of the Sidonians, and after Milcom the abomination of the Ammonites. Solomon did evil in the sight of the LORD, and did not fully follow the LORD, as did his father David. Then Solomon built a high place for Chemosh the abomination of Moab, on the hill that is east of Jerusalem, and for Molech the abomination of the people of Ammon. And he did likewise for all his foreign wives, who burned incense and sacrificed to their gods. So the LORD became angry with Solomon, because his heart had turned from the LORD God of Israel, who had appeared to him twice, and had commanded him concerning this thing, that he should not go after other gods; but he did not keep what the LORD had commanded. Therefore the LORD said to Solomon, "Because you have done this, and have not kept My covenant and My statutes, which I have commanded you, I will surely tear the kingdom away from you and give it to your servant. Nevertheless I will not do it in your days, for the sake of your father David; I will tear it out of the hand of your son. However I will not tear away the whole kingdom; I will give one tribe to your son for the sake of My servant David, and for the sake of Jerusalem which I have chosen."

1 Kings 11:1-13

King Solomon was dubbed the wisest man on earth. Yet with all of his wisdom, Solomon could not rid himself of the *"strange women"* (KJV) he was instructed not to bother with. It wasn't women who were Solomon's problem, but rather strange women. Strange women were in a totally different classification than women. The strange women did not have a covenant with God. They worshipped idol gods that were strictly forbidden. Worse yet was the fact that their entire agenda was to systematically turn Solomon's heart away from the God he served. They would not do this overnight but rather over a period of time, perhaps a dating period.

During this time of intimacy they would get to know the heart of this man so they could twist it. Sexual intimacy is not only a valuable time during which two people who are in covenant come together to share a spiritual and sexual union, but also a time when deception can occur. What I mean by this is that sex in and of itself can be very deceiving since it covers the reality of who a person actually is on the inside. Solomon was blinded to the truth of these women's deceptive patterns and intentions. His intimacy with these strange women caused him to take his focus off of God. Eventually he lost everything that he had fought so hard to achieve.

It is no different today than it was then, in the sense that strange women still have the same motives that they did in Solomon's day, which is to take your eyes away from God. Now let's be honest about something. There is a major difference between a God-fearing woman and a pagan idolatrous woman. The God-fearing woman always has God and His concerns at the top of her list. The ungodly woman never considers God at all. Beyond her lack of acknowledging God, she clearly will do anything she can to separate your union with God because of her jealousy.

You ask, "Well, what if the women Solomon was with were all God-fearing women—would he have been destroyed by the hand of the enemy? Aren't all women capable of being potentially destructive?" The answer is absolutely not. All women are not the same. Even if a God-fearing woman does fall into a sinful encounter because she took her eyes off Christ for a moment, she is still very likely to be reconnected to her first love because she realizes that a moment of pleasure in sin is not comparable to the long-lasting benefits of her relationship with God.

> *By faith Moses, when he became of age, refused to be called the son of Pharaoh's daughter, choosing rather to suffer affliction with the people of God than to enjoy the passing pleasures of sin.*
>
> Hebrews 11:24-25

Let me assure you that the concept of "strange women" is not a gender specific phrase, although it may seem so. There are many strange men as well. Their motive is the same as their female counterparts; it is to try and separate your loving union with God. It is for that reason I've always emphatically emphasized to every single believer that you must never, under any circumstance, date or marry an unbeliever. There are no exceptions to that rule. None!

You rebut, "But he really wants to be saved. He promised me that he was going to come to church with me. He told me that he loves me and that he would do anything that would make me happy." You see, already you've lost the battle. Without even realizing it, you have become the competition of God. And I know that you know that you are obviously no match for Him. When you say things like,

"He'll do it to make me happy," and "He'll do it for me," both of your motives are wrong from the very start. Salvation is never genuine, never pure, when it is done with anyone else in mind other than God and oneself. If he truly desires to be born again, he'll get saved without making any prior contractual agreements with you.

Jesus shed His blood for the forgiveness of sins. He is the One who made the ultimate sacrifice. Shouldn't your salvation be totally predicated on that alone? I would think so. If someone gets born again to please me it will inevitably displease God. It's kind of like going out on a date with an ugly guy only to please your best friend since the guy is her cousin. It is obvious that you neither like the guy nor enjoy his company. The only reason you are doing it is to please her. After that date, it's over! That is the same attitude many unsaved people have about God.

You must never, under any circumstance, date or marry an unbeliever.

They think, *I'll pretend to enjoy all this "God stuff." I'll go along with the whole plan long enough for me to get what I want and get her where I want her to be: far away from God. At that point it really won't matter how much she realizes about my true self and my aversion toward the things of God.* Believe me, that is how they think. So you must be aware in order to maintain godly integrity and loyalty at all times.

Sad to say, I've heard of professing-to-be-saved women who had sex with a glib-talking sinner who said all the right things, only to discover the truth after they became pregnant. I've heard of even more drastic cases of professing Christian women getting caught out with a total sinner, becoming pregnant, and then deciding to marry the man. That is the epitome of stupidity. I did not say that he received Christ; no, he stayed the same sinner that he had always been.

He did not promise to even come to church with her. In fact, he made it very clear that he would never come to her church no matter what. Totally blinded, she married the fool anyhow. Although she has recommitted her life back to the Lord and is serving God with a greater conviction, she still has to deal with the consequences of her foolish past choices that continue to plague her until this very day.

I've heard sinner guys make dumb remarks such as, "I am the devil. I'm Satan incarnate." Or worse yet, "I am God." Then I saw gullible women laugh at their ridiculous annotations, not even realizing that those kinds of statements should have been the greatest turn-off to them. Here is the truth to remember: When you play with the devil long enough, you become very de-sensitized to his conversation and his personality. Things that should bother you about the devil tend not to bother you as much as they used to. When that starts to happen, you should immediately begin to inspect yourself to make sure that you are still in the faith.

Your walk with God should never pose a conflict to yourself—only to the kingdom of darkness. Solomon's reign was marked by a continual struggle between two conflicting orientations: faithfulness to his God and fulfillment of the Judaic religious teachings versus insidious strange influences that penetrated the kingdom and that made demands on his body, soul, and spirit. Because of his political marriages to these foreign women, Solomon was compelled to

accept their cultural practices, many of which were in dia-
metrical opposition to the kingdom of the God of Israel.

In time, his influence would wane tremendously. The sad
part is that he did not realize it until it was far too late. That
is the way the enemy gets you into his world—by testing
your love toward God and His church on smaller things,
then larger, then grandiose. I've seen both men and women
do this. "Why do you have to go to church all the time? Let's
go the beach. Next Sunday, let's go out of town. The Sunday
after that, I'm taking you to Vegas."

The whole focus is not to spend more quality time with
you but to get your entire life totally distracted from the things
of God. It's to make you become weakened. The whole idea
is to get you so far away from the Word that you literally have
no strength at all. Then when Satan comes against you to
attack you, you don't have any strength to resist him.
Eventually Satan will kill you without your seeing it coming.
No matter how you slice it, Christians should never be in
union with unbelievers. No matter how hard you try to make
it work, it will never work. God never designed it to work.

TRYING TO BALANCE THE SEESAW

*Do not be unequally yoked together with unbeliev-
ers. For what fellowship has righteousness with law-
lessness? And what communion has light with darkness? And what accord has Christ with Belial? Or
what part has a believer with an unbeliever? And
what agreement has the temple of God with idols?
For you are the temple of the living God. As God has
said: "I will dwell in them and walk among them. I*

will be their God, and they shall be My people."
Therefore "Come out from among them and be sepa-
rate, says the Lord. Do not touch what is unclean,
and I will receive you. I will be a Father to you, and
you shall be My sons and daughters, says the LORD
Almighty."

2 Corinthians 6:14-18

God gives the command (not suggestion) not to be
unequally yoked for a very specific reason. He knows that an
unequally yoked relationship is bound for failure. So it would
save a great amount of time and heartache to avoid getting
involved with one to begin with. So many more marriages are
being destroyed for ignoring this principle that the numbers
are becoming more alarming as they increase. Equally as
alarming is the damage done to the lives of single young
Christians who venture into this dangerous arena of courting
pagans. No matter how hard you try to make it work, the bottom line is it won't. It was never meant to be in the first place.

The saved person and the sinner were never meant to be
with one another in a spiritually workable companionship.
Being unequally yoked is like having an obese child who
weighs about 245 pounds play on the seesaw with a 50-
pound seven-year-old. The seesaw will be imbalanced from
the very beginning; it won't move until the overweight child
gets off the seesaw. It won't make any difference how much
the two kids like each other and how great they get along.
One puts the other totally off balance.

No matter how hard you try, you simply cannot force what
God has never ordained. Some things in life were designed to

work with one another. It's the way He created them. They were not forced to work, but rather they evolved out of a natural progression. For example, a sperm and an egg are designed to work with each other. If two sperms or two eggs come together it would be biologically and molecularly impossible for them to become fertilized. Only a sperm and an egg can produce an embryo. No matter what you try to do to change that process, it will remain the same.

You cannot force what God has never ordained.

What about a lock and a key? There is a key that is specifically designed to fit a particular lock. You can't use that key on any other lock and expect it to open. It only works with the one that it was designed for. There are many keys that look extremely similar yet are different. You will know that they are different once you try to use a key on a lock that it was not designed for.

How about a fish in relation to water? Fish were created to live in the water. That is their natural habitat. I'm not a betting man, but if I were I would bet that you probably have never seen a fish walking on land before. Of course you haven't. Land is not a natural fit for fish. Most fish dread living on land. When on land they are usually stuffed, broiled, sautéed, or fried. If you were a fish I don't think you would look forward to frequent land visits either.

Once they are taken out of the water, fish immediately begin to gasp for breath. They begin to die when they are not in the place designed for them. You are no different than they are in the sense that you too begin to slowly die and deteriorate when you are taken out of the arena God has called you to prosper in. Although the two-parent household is nearly obsolete, it is still God's best for a mother and father to be in the home raising their children. That is the way God designed it.

> *Listen to your father who begot you, and do not despise your mother when she is old.*

> Proverbs 23:22

This verse and many others corroborate the point that God intended for the father and mother to be the set people whom their children use as master models. I realize that when you look around within our society, things are really not going according to God's original plans. But that's the point. That is the sole reason there are so many young people without proper role models, guidance, and direction. For the most part fathers have forfeited their responsibilities to their sons, leaving them to fend for themselves.

Most fathers are not there. I don't mean that they are not in the home. You could actually live with your child and yet not be there. When I say that they are not there, I literally mean that most children don't even know who their father is. For the few who do know who their dads are, often their dads aren't very responsible to teach them anything of lasting value. This only leaves them with no other alternative than to repeat a generational cycle of perpetual self-defeating behavior.

A husband and wife were designed to work best with each other. Now I realize that every husband and wife couple doesn't necessarily work out the best. I also realize that more and more single mothers are having to bear the total responsibility of rearing their children, feeding them, clothing them, sheltering them, educating them, and bringing them up in the ways of the Lord. Both you and I know that is far too much pressure to put on a woman.

When the mother and father work collectively to raise the child (whether they live together or not) God supernaturally causes favor to come upon your agreement. The child ends up being a productive asset to society rather than another incarcerated felon. It all begins with understanding that when two things are designed to work together, trying to forcefully employ another method simply will not work. And even if it does work functionally, it will not work optimally. In other words, it won't be God's best.

The only thing that an unbeliever and a believer have in common is their sexual organs.

My concern is that too many Christian people take this whole thing far too lightly. As a result, the body of Christ, the family, and the nation have suffered greatly. Believers were not designed to be with unbelievers. It is totally unnatural. They do not think the same. They do not have the same ideals, values, or spiritual convictions. The only thing that an unbeliever and a believer have in common is their sexual organs.

And that is usually about as shallow as the relationship stays. Think about it. What can an unsaved man or woman say to you or about you that will make you get excited or turned on? Face it, they know nothing about the realm of the spirit. They don't know about the joy of the Lord. They've neither been introduced to nor been able to practice the fruit of the Spirit. They cannot practice purity or the presence of the Lord. So they are forced to deal with you in every way on a totally carnal level.

They cannot sufficiently compliment your spiritual character because they don't understand it. That forces them to talk about your body parts, your appendages, and your very pronounced yet sexy features. Since they cannot converse about spiritual things with you, you will inevitably be forced to decrease your standard and talk their low-life, cheap talk simply to appease them. Every conceivable corruption enters in the house of God through the pagan/Christian union. The devil realizes that he has no welcomed way into the house of the Lord unless a Christian invites him. Make sure that you are not the one giving the devil a personal invitation. It will cost you far more than you are willing to pay.

ENDNOTE

1. *Merriam Webster's Unabridged Dictionary*, 3.0 (Merriam-Webster Incorporated, 2003), "romance."

Chapter Five

PROTECTED AND UNPROTECTED SEX

————⟫●⟪————

The very first thing most people think of when they hear the phrase *unprotected sex* is how they can enjoy the pleasures of sexual intimacy without having to deal with the possibilities of potential sexually transmitted diseases such as venereal diseases and AIDS. The Trojan company spends multiple millions of dollars on advertising to convince their clientele to use their ever-improving condoms. They boast that if you are a woman and your partner uses a condom, you will have a 99 percent chance of not getting pregnant.

If you are a man they make you feel pretty certain that you won't get a sexually contracted disease. So the bottom line is that they make you feel pretty secure if you wear their products; you will be safe, unaffected, and for the most part protected from any life-altering concerns. But what they don't disclose to you is that far more may be transferred in the act of sex than their rubber Trojans could ever bar from entering into your spirit.

So to that end, in this chapter we will talk straightforward about sex. Sex is one of those topics that conventional and classical Christianity shy away from. They shy away from it so much that it is one of the main things that have become totally out of control within the church. While the church continues to point their finger at the world and all their sins, the world looks directly at the church and laughs out loud to see that the church also is dealing with the same issues that the world is.

Often people of the world will say, "The reason I really don't want to go to church is because I don't want to be a hypocrite." They'll confess, "I'm not ready to make that kind of commitment right now." I've heard them say, "I see church people at the same nightclubs I go to, trying to pick up guys just like me. So if I'm going to be doing this, I really don't want to be in church faking like those phonies. I'm sexing and they are too. There is no real difference between the two of us."

Sad to say, this is the overall mind-set and view of many sinners today. The real truth is that we in the church can't keep silent anymore. The church has done a remarkably horrible job of dealing with the sex issue. From one side they've condemned the very act of sex so vehemently that even many saved married people feel limited in exploration within their beds of intimacy. Some married women who are saved (especially those who hold puritanical beliefs sacred) sincerely believe that sex is really a "necessary nasty" thing to do primarily for the purpose of bearing children.

The church is much to blame for this since it is the original institution that gave society an image of sexuality in the first place. The problem is that the image that the church gave society is so far from God's views on sex that it is literally shameful. Nowhere in the Scriptures will you ever find sex, particularly in the confines of marriage, to be looked on as filthy or nasty. Even outside of the boundaries of marriage sex is still an enjoyable experience. Now don't go running away with that statement. Both you and I realize that outside of the confines of marriage having sex can have very negative consequences despite how good it feels.

God never intended sex to be a dirty word.

The point is that sex was never intended by God to be a dirty word. Like many other things, we have once again allowed the world to take what was intended to be used for God's glory and pervert it. If you go to most churches around the world, you will hear preachers preach hell, fire, and brimstone messages against people who are having sex. They'll say, "Sex is a sin." Think about it. If you hear someone preaching and ranting on about how sinful sex is, you are more than likely going to do one of three things.

The first thing you will be inclined to do is abstain from sex altogether. In other words, you will freely choose to never have sex in your entire life with anyone anywhere. That's an option. However, it is not the option that most people choose unless you are a nun or a Trappist monk. The second inclination will be to totally avoid the church altogether and continue to live the lifestyle that you choose. Unfortunately, this is the deadly option that the vast majority chooses.

The third option is that you become submitted to God's Word and allow His Word to sanctify your body, mind, and spirit. You allow God's Word to totally define you and establish you in your vocation, making your life so focused on your purpose that nothing else can get in the way of your destiny. Obviously, this option is the best of all three; however, it is the road less traveled. So in this chapter I want to try to get more people back on the road less traveled, toward their victory.

S-E-X IS NOT A FOUR-LETTER WORD

Sex is not a sin. Sex is not dirty and nasty. Sex is not vulgar. All those negative things and many more have been attributed to the word *sex*. What many people fail to recognize is that sex is not a demonic thought or creation. Sex has always been God's idea. It has been in His mind and on His mind before He began the beginnings. Everything that is and that will ever be in mammal form came through sexual intimacy.

God created sex not only for the purpose of multiplying on the earth, but also for the purpose of enjoyment and recreation. Just look at the word *re-creation*. *Re* means again or to repeat. *Create* means to bring into existence, to make out of nothing. Thus two people having sexual intimacy have the ability to bring things into existence over and over again. So if sexual intimacy has the potential to cause people to create things over and over, then like many things, sex can be used as a tool to promote good or evil.

Realizing that, then whatever you create in the moment of your sexual passion will ultimately proliferate itself many times over. For example, if two persons are married and have intimate sexual relations, they create a child. That child—given the right rearing, love, and atmosphere—will be inclined to produce more children like him or herself. Long before that child becomes an adult, he or she will have created (in an attractive sense) friends compatible for him or her, since everything produces after its own kind.

What you create in the moment of your sexual passion will ultimately proliferate itself many times over.

On the other hand, if two persons, let's say single persons, have sexual intimacy outside the boundaries of a genuine commitment, whatever is created under those compromising circumstances will spread like an infectious disease. Perhaps you may wonder what I mean by "genuine commitment." Allow me to explain. A genuine commitment is when two people are in total agreement on the conditions and terms of the relationship and are totally committed to upholding the value that each party knows will eventually bring about good success in each other's lives. That applies to every area of each other's lives.

This applies not only to singles but also to married people. There are many people who are married yet not genuinely committed. Now I do not mean that either party has been unfaithful to the other. My point goes deeper than that. You can be faithful to your partner yet still be uncommitted to his or her overall development and progress in life. I've seen unsaved men who are married to Christian wives never attempt to accompany their wives to church or support their spiritual values. Although the man is married to his wife in a legal sense, he has still broken his commitment to her, particularly the vows that bind them to a lifelong commitment of enhancing each other in all ways, including spiritually.

People who have low self-esteem and harbor ill feelings from the past tend to birth those same characteristics in those whom they are sexually intimate with. I don't believe it would be stretching it too far to say that illicit sexual behavioral patterns, alternate lifestyles, schizophrenia, mental instability, and demonic oppression are all easily transferable to the person who does not protect him or herself from these anti-Christian influences.

The bottom line is that you will receive the same spirit of the person you are intimately engaged with. (We'll touch on this further later in the chapter.) So you need to be both careful and prayerful. Now for some, that may be a pretty hard truth to accept, considering just how indiscreet you were in your unregenerated days; nonetheless, it is still true. I've even seen women—both married and single—who unknowingly slept with a man who was a child molester and the contrary spirit on that man transferred into them. Now you may think, *That's not fair to say that. You can't say that just because a person had sex with a child molester that he or she too will become a child molester.*

That is not what I am saying. What I am saying is that even in that sad situation, the person who was intimate with the child molester may develop the propensity to accept or tolerate that partner's wicked sin. I've witnessed people in this unfortunate predicament actually taking up for the child molester, making excuses for the person and his (or her) harmful behavior. The woman will say, "He really didn't know what he was doing. He never really wanted to hurt anyone. His father molested him when he was a child. My husband was never properly loved when he was growing up." The list of excuses can go on forever. What this woman does not realize is that she has become tolerant of his sinful ways through the sexual/spiritual exchange.

It is not much different when you look at how some women allow men to abuse them, neglect them, and cause harm to their children even though they are not married to those men (not that marriage is a reason to allow such abuse either). The reason they tolerate very apparent abuse is because they, through sexual intercourse, have become de-sensitized to that kind of behavior. Although they know that, conventionally speaking as well as biblically and morally speaking, the behavior is simply wrong, they continue to tolerate it because they have an "installed" acceptance toward it. You can look at this in terms of computer software for an even clearer example.

The computer on which I write books cannot function without an operating system such as Microsoft ®Windows ®XP. Microsoft ®Windows ®XP gives the computer not only a life but also a vehicle to operate on. It kind of gives it permission to do whatever you need to do on your computer. Without it, your personal computer cannot work at all. Using that same train of thought, you and I can give our permission to another person's permissiveness and improprieties by lending our bodies as the operating system that makes the enemy work and function optimally. Without your consent the bad guy has nothing to work through. So for all intents and purposes, you need to realize that you have the ability to close that door once and for all. Quite obviously that choice is up to you.

God designed sex to be a beautiful experience shared by two individuals who are biblically committed to one another. I have to clarify "biblically committed" for your understanding. I fully realize that we live in an era where any and everything goes. Some people believe that by being in a relationship for a couple of years or more that they qualify as being married. People have taken the phrase *common law marriage* totally out of context, having no idea what it really means. I'll talk more about that in Chapter Six, "The Raw Truth About Shacking Up."

For now, realize that you are responsible for protecting yourself, your image, and your body, mind, and soul from outside influences as best as possible. However, in the process of doing that, don't look down on sex as if it is something dirty and nasty or as something to be avoided for the rest of your life. You don't have to be paranoid; you just need to use your spiritual sense. Be led by your spirit not by your flesh, and in so doing you will please the Father and avoid a whole lot of senseless trouble.

It is the Spirit who gives life; the flesh profits nothing. The words that I speak to you are spirit, and they are life.

John 6:63

BLESSED IS THE MAN WHOSE SINS ARE COVERED

Blessed is he whose transgression is forgiven, whose sin is covered. Blessed is the man to whom the LORD does not impute iniquity, and in whose spirit there is no deceit.

Psalm 32:1-2

Okay, you may be thinking to yourself, *I've already got into relational trouble,* and you are wondering if there is any real hope for you. Perhaps you are in the middle of a very compromising situation right now and you can't see a clear pathway out. Or you may be like the masses of people that fall into sin and foolishly believe God hates them and no longer wants to have anything to do with them at all. The Bible tells us that the person whose sins are covered should consider him or herself very blessed.

It is obvious why such people should consider themselves to be blessed if their sins are covered. If your sins are covered then you do not have to pay the ultimate penalty for your sin. The ultimate penalty for sin, no matter which way it is delivered, is always death. Now I realize that in some barbaric cultures still existing today people still employ the death penalty for all criminal offenders and for those who break moral and cultural traditions. But for the most part, in a "virtually civilized" society, most people are not immediately killed based on a sin committed.

Most people, whether they realize it or not, are given a major grace period—or should I say an amazing grace period—whereby they can get things straightened out. But all this favor and grace is only made possible by and through the price paid by the Lord Jesus Christ in His sacrificial death on the cross. The blood that He shed makes it possible for us to receive God's forgiveness and for our sins to be covered by that same blood.

You must realize, though, that there is a distinct difference between hiding someone's sin and covering it. When you try to hide a sin, it is bound to be exposed because sin has a clever way of working itself to the surface. The scripture in Psalm 32 does not say blessed is the man whose sins are hidden. You can hide behind a bush, but if the bush is removed then you will be exposed. Or if your body is far larger than the width of the bush, you'll still be seen on the left and right sides of the bush since the bush won't be large enough to conceal you.

When I was a child, I used to play a game I'm sure you are familiar with: "hide and go seek." The whole object of the game was for me to go and hide and my friends to come and find me. I would have to hide in a place that was not conspicuous at all. If I were in the house, I'd hide under the bed or in the closet in the hopes that I would not be discovered.

If I were outside, I would hide behind a tree or perhaps even climb up in the tree. No matter where I would hide, though, I would always be found by somebody who was looking for me. The few times when I would hide well enough so that no one could find me for a while, I'd end up exposing my own self by running toward my friends shouting, "You couldn't find me."

Although I felt really big that they could not find me, my whereabouts would always eventually be revealed. Why was that? You cannot continue to hide anything forever. If no one exposes you, you'll expose yourself without even realizing it. But when God covers you with the blood of Christ, there is no need to be exposed. His blood does such a fine job of cleansing you that no one could ever see the remnant of your past indulgences.

That is why a person who used to be a prostitute, who has submitted him or herself to Jesus, can no longer be looked at based on his or her wanton past actions. The only thing that you and I can see is a man or woman who reflects the glory of Christ the King. His or her sin was not hidden; rather, it no longer exists. People whose sins are covered have made a conscientious choice to surrender their will to

When God covers you with the blood of Christ, there is no need for past sin to be exposed.

God's will. They have made a decision not to allow their past or present actions to sabotage their future. And so, they ask God to cover them so that the stain of their negative choices won't be apparent at all. Thank God for that!

DAVID'S SIN WAS COVERED

In this particular psalm, Psalm 32, David expressed his extreme gratefulness at having received a full pardon for the sin of coveting after and having sexual intercourse with another man's wife. David was not just any common individual in the kingdom; he was the king. If anyone should have known exactly what to do or not to do as far as protocol and godly living were concerned, it should have been King David. In fact, during this time many kings and possibly King David also were actively involved in the lawmaking process that governed the region in which they ruled over. So David's unfounded actions further prove to us that even the best of us may fall or fail if we lose sight of our prioritized focus.

For the commoner, this transgression that David committed would have had a hefty consequence: death by stoning. For a king, the consequences should have been far more severe if that were at all possible. However, because David's heart was in the right place, his life was spared and he was given a second chance to make good on his life's assignment. His sin was covered. Because of that he was able to maintain his position in the kingdom, but more importantly, he continued to maintain his proper place in the life of God.

Unfortunately, David's first child born from this union died far too prematurely. However, God was not being vindictive, playing a "tit for a tat" with David in this matter. David was an accessory to the crime of murder. And murder will always be punished since it represents the shedding of blood, something that no man has the moral right to do. The murder of an innocent man is even more wrong, particularly since the blood he shed will not redeem anything of worthwhile value. There is no even exchange.

These six things the LORD hates, yes, seven are an abomination to Him: a proud look, a lying tongue, **hands that shed innocent blood.**

Proverbs 6:16-17, emphasis added

Any person who does not have to pay for his or her own sins is blessed. Just to know that your foolish choices are not credited on your lifelong tab but have been paid in full by a generous Man should make you feel all the more excited about His covering. Let me warn you, though, that if you consciously continue to live your life so recklessly after having received Jesus Christ, you may be forgiven but you may be deprived of His covering.

The old folks coined a phrase that said, "The Lord helps those who help themselves." Although God is all-powerful, you can still limit His ability to cover you when you continual- *does not have to pay* ly choose to walk out from under the place where He cov- *for his or her own* ers. Think about if it was rain- ing like cats and dogs outside *sins is blessed.* and you chose not to stay under the covering of an umbrella. Is it the umbrella's fault for not covering you? Or does the blame rest on you for removing yourself from the permanent covering of the umbrella? I think the answer is quite obvious. Stay wherever you are being properly covered. People who will cover for you accurately represent the qualities and nature of the Lord Jesus Christ.

Any person who does not have to pay for his or her own sins is blessed.

That is why it is so important, and I'll continue to stress this point over and over again, that single people need to submit to their pastor as their covering. The enemy is so eager and persistent to ruin the lives of single saints because he realizes their amazing potential to impact the world for Christ. His primary way of access to most single people is when they are not covered by a man or woman of God. The devil can't get to you on God's territory, only on his. That is why the church is so extremely important. That is why a praying and purpose-oriented church is so vital. It represents the umbrella in which you can run under for safety from the coming storms. Don't for one moment allow yourself not to be covered by a spiritual authority. Where you are not being properly covered is where the devil will surely destroy you.

WHOSE SPIRIT DO YOU HAVE?

Let's talk about a phrase that has been getting a lot of attention in recent years in the body of Christ, called "the transference of spirits." One of the things that may not be taught on in depth within the church at large is exactly what happens when two people have sex with one another. Okay, let's bypass all the good stuff connected to sex (the pleasurable feeling, the sensational emotions, and the sense of being loved) and get right down to the real deal.

What exactly is "the transference of spirits" and how does such a transfer take place when two people have sex with one another? First, "the transference of spirits" is a literal transference of a particular spirit into your body. For example, lust, poverty, child molestation, homosexuality, drug addiction, alcoholism, and hate are all spirits that can be transferred from one person to another. They are like communicable diseases. People who are infected with diseases that can easily spread are usually quarantined in order to keep the disease from spreading any further.

One well-known way that spirits are transferred can be best explained in a biblical doctrine called, "the laying on of hands." In this process a person literally lays hands on another person and transmits what he has into the recipient. The Bible shows various examples of this. One example is when Jesus had already ascended back to heaven. Peter and John, both His disciples, laid hands on the new believers who were expecting to receive the baptism in the Holy Spirit. The Holy Spirit on Peter and John was transferable, so much so that as soon as they laid hands on the people they were filled with the Holy Spirit, or the Spirit of Christ, on the inside.

Then they laid hands on them, and they received the Holy Spirit. And when Simon saw that through the laying on of the apostles' hands the Holy Spirit was given, he offered them money, saying, "Give me this power also, that anyone on whom I lay hands may receive the Holy Spirit."

Acts 8:17-19

From this example we can safely gather that whatever is on you can get on someone else, particularly in a spiritual sense. So then demon spirits are transferable just as easily as godly and righteous spirits are transferable. Remember that whatever is on someone can be transferred to another, whether good or bad.

One day Jesus went into a certain city to conduct a miracle and healing crusade. No matter what He did, the people en masse could not receive their healing because of their unbelief. It is quite interesting to note that the spirit of unbelief that was on the people was so strong that it interrupted the flow of healing in Jesus.

Now He could do no mighty work there, except that He laid His hands on a few sick people and healed them.

Mark 6:5

It literally short-circuited the flow of God to them. As with any crowd of people, you will always find a small group of maybe one or two persons within that crowd who is willing to take God at His Word. You will always have those who are willing to release their faith for the miraculous to occur.

Such was the case in this crowd. There was a minority of people who believed on Jesus. Jesus laid His hands on these few people, and they were healed. The healing power of Jesus was transferred to the sick and diseased through the laying on of His hands.

> *When He had come to the other side, to the country of the Gergesenes, there met Him two demon-possessed men, coming out of the tombs, exceedingly fierce, so that no one could pass that way. And suddenly they cried out, saying, "What have we to do with You, Jesus, You Son of God? Have You come here to torment us before the time?" Now a good way off from them there was a herd of many swine feeding. So the demons begged Him, saying, "If You cast us out, permit us to go away into the herd of swine." And He said to them, "Go." So when they had come out, they went into the herd of swine. And suddenly the whole herd of swine ran violently down the steep place into the sea, and perished in the water. Then those who kept them fled; and they went away into the city and told everything, including what had happened to the demon-possessed men. And behold, the whole city came out to meet Jesus. And when they saw Him, they begged Him to depart from their region.*

> Matthew 8:28-34

In the story above Jesus cast a demon out of two demon-possessed men. When He did, the demons went into the pigs that were nearby, causing them to drown in the water. The message in this story is unmistakable: "Stay clear of demons; they will try to influence whomever is nearby!" Demons have to have somewhere to go. Demons themselves will be tormented if they don't have a place to live. They'll be forced to live in the air. And they cannot do as much harm as they would like to do if they are living in the air or the atmosphere. They must have a body to occupy.

If a spirit can be transferred by the laying on of hands, how much more can it be transferred when two people have sex?

The reason I mentioned the ways that spirits can be transferred was to make a valid point. If a spirit can be transferred by laying hands on someone's body, by laying hands on your clothes, or by commanding the spirit with words to leave and not come back, how much more would a spirit be communicated when two people are having sexual intercourse?

You would not believe just how many spirits are picked up when people have sex. That is where the entire concept of covering begins to play an even more significant role. God has territory. However, He also has allowed the devil to have temporary control over certain territories. If a believer willingly chooses to enter into that territory without God's consent and leading, then that person is totally on his or her own. He or she has allowed him or herself to be uncovered and unprotected from the wicked plans of the enemy to kill, steal, and destroy.

Sex is ultimately an exchange between two individuals. So whatever is on your partner will inevitably get transferred to you. I know that may sound pretty horrible to some, but unfortunately there are so many who "casually sex" or "socially sex" that they never take the time to find out anything about the person with whom they are intimate. I know of single people who have had sex with people they don't even know the basics about. They shared their God-given virtue with a person whose name, street address, city, state, and zip code they didn't even know.

For a million-dollar vow they could not tell you whether the person loved God or worshipped Satan. They could not tell you if the person respected his or her parents, loved children, worked a job, or was a notorious thief. So you can see how easily a negative and ungodly spirit can be transferred without someone even knowing it. What I want you to realize is that the enemy's job is to keep you totally ignorant of truth. His job is to convince you of a total lie. He wants to make you believe that you can continue to make the fleshy choices that you've been making and that you will prosper regardless.

Perhaps I may write about this in a future edition, but if I were to take a statistical survey on the aftereffects of singles who give into each other sexually, I'm pretty certain that the majority would not only express their deepest regrets for their decision but also admit that they never would have believed that it would turn out that way. Think about it. No one just expects to have sex and get a disease such as AIDS or herpes. At least intelligent-thinking people don't expect such things.

Everybody gets into it with the highest expectations, only to be totally mistaken. Far more is transferred into you than just a physical disease. There are millions of people walking around the earth with spiritual AIDS, having been infected by a carrier of the trait. Similar to the disease that we know of, spiritual AIDS attacks your spiritual health, your spiritual immune system, and your ability to make spiritually rational decisions. It attacks and destroys your dreams, visions, and goals. It wars against your purpose and totally retards your progress and overall development.

I'm quite sure that had you known all those realities could be transferred into your spirit, you would have thought longer before you made the choice to allow someone to *lay hands* on you. The good news is that it's not over. Even if you've already allowed the wrong person to lay his or her hands on you, you can reverse the effects of the transfer by inviting Christ to lay His hands on you and infusing His Spirit within you. Cancel the enemy's plans for your life right now! Take back your life, reclaim your future, and begin living the God-kind of life that He always intended for you.

NOWHERE TO HIDE

Where can I go from Your Spirit? Or where can I flee from Your presence? If I ascend into heaven, You are there; if I make my bed in hell, behold, You are there. If I take the wings of the morning, and dwell in the uttermost parts of the sea, even there Your hand shall lead me, and Your right hand shall hold me. If I say, "Surely the darkness shall fall on me," even the night shall be light about me; indeed, the darkness shall not hide from You, but the night shines as the day; the darkness and the light are both alike to You.

Psalm 139:7-12

You can run but you can't hide. And that's a good thing. There is really no need to run away from God after you've failed. In fact, you should do just the opposite. You should run toward Him. The enemy has done an intentionally good job of confusing believers as to how they should respond when they get in a situation of compromise or experience breakdown.

The devil makes you believe that if you hide away from the people of God, stay away from *You can run* church, and don't do anything remotely spiritual, that you are home free. But *but you can't* that is simply not true. According to Psalm 139:7-12, no matter where you *hide.* decide to go God is already there. You cannot hide from God. Even if you decide to hide in hell, God is there too. God is everywhere at the same time. He is omnipresent.

I know that since you were a small child you were taught that God lives in the sky. That is only true in part. God could never make the skies His sole dwelling place. If so, He would be able to be contained by the skies, thus subjecting Him to boundaries. And that cannot happen because God is limitless. He has no boundaries. You must accept the truth that God's most comfortable dwelling place of choice is inside your heart.

So stop trying to escape your guilt. Please stop trying to escape godly conviction. Godly conviction is a very normal thing to feel. You ought to be glad that the spirit of conviction comes upon you. It is a sign that God's Spirit has not left you. That is a wonderful thing. Don't get mad that you feel remorse over your bad choices. That only proves that you are still intimately connected to God. If you were not connected, you would not feel anything.

One thing that was true about David is that he did not hide from God. When David got into trouble or failed God, he would never run from God; rather he ran toward God. Stop hiding. God's not mad at you. In fact, He just wants to restore you as soon as possible. No matter what the situation, He loves you. God is at home with you when you choose not to attend church. God is there after you've sinned. And He is also there when you desire to come clean. Unlike you and me, God does not hold grudges. So stop trying to hide from Him. Run toward God and get the cleansing you so desperately need.

Do not cast me away from Your presence, and do not take Your Holy Spirit from me.

Psalm 51:11

RECEIVING THE FATHER'S CLEANSING LOVE

If we confess our sins, He is faithful and just to forgive us our sins and to cleanse us from all unrighteousness. If we say that we have not sinned, we make Him a liar, and His word is not in us.

1 John 1:9-10

I could not end this chapter without informing you that God loves you more than you will ever know. I do not want you to feel as if God is throwing you away. God wants to cleanse you. However, your cleansing begins with first acknowledging that you have sin and desperately need to be cleansed by His blood. It doesn't matter who you are or what you have done, God will make you pure.

I've had my share of being around a host of super-sanctimonious saints who eagerly try to convince their hearer that they are without sin. The funny thing is that God's Word says just the opposite. In fact, the Bible says that if you say you are without sin, you are a liar. Not only are you a liar, but you are really declaring that you have no need for Jesus. After all, if you can keep yourself holy and pure in God's eyes, then you don't need Him as a cleansing agent.

If you confess your sins God *will* forgive you. But He won't stop there. God also will cleanse you from all unrighteousness; He'll cleanse you from the aftermath of your actions.

Right now say this prayer:

"Father, I have done some things that I realize I should have never done. I have allowed the enemy to have control over certain areas of my life that should have been solely reserved for You. I realize that I've subjected my body to spiritual abuse and ungodly exposure. I am asking for Your forgiveness for my sin. Please cleanse me and erase the very thought of my sinful past, in Jesus' name. Amen."

Repeat this prayer as often as needed.

Chapter Six

THE RAW TRUTH
ABOUT SHACKING UP

———————

What is shacking up? "Shacking up" is merely a direct street term that quickly describes a man and woman who live together as husband and wife yet refuse to marry one another. A fancy term to describe this arrangement is also *cohabitation*. The old folks used to call it "playing house." Although just 30 or 40 years ago shacking up was shunned and pretty much condemned by society, today it has become a welcomed alternative to marriage. It's such a sad delusion from the enemy because most people who shack up with one another do it so long that they begin to believe that they are married. And if you believe that you are already married when you are not, then there is no reason to actually go ahead and do the real thing.

Shacking up is not only a major deception but also a gross and intentional undermining of God's original plan for the family, which consists of a husband and wife. Sad to say, living together is not really looked down upon like it used to be years ago. As a result there is no external societal pressure impressed on the shackers to even want to get married. I imagine that our culture has become anesthetized to any and everything that opposes the principles set forth in God's Word.

People refer to their lovers as wife or husband even though they are not married to them. And family, friends, and first-time associates just accept it as totally normal. The sad thing is that they are still just as single as can be but don't even realize it. If you think that this problem is a small one, think again. According to a recent statistical survey on cohabitation, Americans lead the pack in the area of shacking.

1. Percentage of Americans who have cohabited at one time or another: 50%

2. Percentage of cohabiting couples who go on to marry: 50-60%

3. Percentage of cohabiting relationships involving children: 40%

4. Percentage of unions that survive two years: Cohabiting unions not leading to marriage: 33% Marital unions: 95%

5. Percentage of unions that survive ten years: Cohabiting unions not leading to marriage: 12% Marital unions: 90%

6. Likelihood of divorce within first ten years of marriage: Those who cohabit prior to marriage are almost

twice as likely to divorce as opposed to those who do not cohabit prior to marriage.[1]

You may ask, "What's the big deal? I don't see anything wrong with it at all." Most men who choose to shack rather than wed say, "I've got to test the waters first, to see if I actually want to spend the rest of my life with this woman. My momma didn't raise no fool and I ain't gonna say I do, when deep down within, I know that I don't.'' "After all, most large purchases in life always are preceded by a test run. No one buys a new car without first test driving the car. In fact, the higher end luxury automobile dealers, like Lexus, Mercedes, and Maserati may even allow you to take the car home for the weekend for a trial spin."

You may think that the above mock dialog is just "off the wall" rhetoric, but in all actuality it isn't. Lots of men really think that low. They really believe that a woman is not much better than a nicely detailed car, a computer with a whole lot of hard drive space or season tickets to the New York Giants or the New York Mets. The more unfortunate tragedy is that most women acquiesce to men's insensitive nature. And when women agree to this, they only help to perpetuate an ongoing cycle that has caused more damage than good.

Yet you still wonder why the big deal? You may feel as if no one is being affected by your choice to obscure your single life by shacking up with someone. Perhaps you believe that if anyone can possibly be affected by your choice, it could never be anyone other than you and your significant other. Not so! There are many people who are directly or indirectly affected by your choice to play house. Beyond that there are many things that happen that you may not have realized before when you chose this path. Below I have listed five subtitles that deal with what actually happens when you choose to cohabit. Keep reading.

UNDERMINING GOD

One of the first things that happen when you choose to cohabit is that you undermine God's plan for your life and His original plan for the family. Although it may sound a bit dated and may not be very popular these days, God still desires that we follow His plan, His original plan for the family. Another way of looking at this is to realize that God has set forth a pattern for the establishment of family. Family and procreation should happen within the context of marriage. Quite obviously this God-idea is not the conventionally accepted idea of most people in society, which is the main reason there are so many kids being born to unwed parents.

God, not society, is the One who set forth the pattern for the establishment of family.

Now before you go ahead and start judging me, thinking that I am judging you, wait just a minute. I am not even mentioning this topic with the least bit of judgment in mind. I am only bringing this whole topic up to communicate the heart of God concerning the matter and to offer a viable solution to the problem that plagues our society. Let's face it; we live in a generation of lawless children and parents. Babies (in a figurative sense) are giving birth to babies, not having any clue how to take care of them.

Little kids who have not even grown up, finished high school, or attempted college, feel big and bad enough to tackle the vicissitudes of life, having no road map to where they are going. If this were a remote circumstance, it would be one thing. But this popular trend is fast growing. This is not how God intended for it to be. When a man and a woman live together as if they are married, it superimposes their thoughts over God's thoughts about marriage and the family. They are saying, "God, I realize that You invented the family and gave us a manual on how it should run, but I think my idea is far better than Your idea."

You are basically telling God that He was unknowledgeable on how He created family to begin with. Our society is always making one attempt after another to try to redefine the family and marriage. Think about it, could you imagine someone trying to redefine words like *money, law, congress, sex, medical doctor, politician,* or even the *President of the United States?* Absolutely not! Those words and terms already have a meaning that is not only workable but also purposeful. That makes all the difference in the world.

Consider the fact that, historically, African-American people as well as women were not considered whole persons. They were not looked on or treated as equals but rather as a percentage of a whole person—maybe 1/3, 1/2, or 5/8. In that case, mankind made an error to begin with in trying to define something that already had an established definition. God made men and women whole and equal. For someone to try to re-determine that definition would be nonsensical. Although sexism and racism have lasted even until this day and caused many people not to be able to compete on a global market, it's still wrong.

Even though the family unit has been redefined by society and even by our court system, God's definition will still prevail. After all, it is God who created the family. It would only make sense that He should have the last say on classifying His own creation. Bill Gates defines Microsoft since it is his creation. When we try to rework God's ideas, it never lasts. It may appear to work for a moment, but in time it's bound to fail. That is one of the main reasons cohabitation never works. It was never intended to work. And when we undermine God's plan, we should never expect His favor.

CREATING A FALSE ILLUSION

Another thing that cohabiting creates is a false illusion. It creates the look of marriage when in fact it is not marriage. It creates the look of a family but is not family at all. It creates the look of building a future together, but in a few months to a year, the fantasy ride comes to a complete crashing stop. If you are a man and you truly love the woman you are living with, why not marry her?

Why would you believe that continuing in that vein could ever be promising? Ladies, why would you rather have an illusion than what is real? Why not just continue to date? The home should be a place where both the king and the queen rule together. If your living situation compromises that ethic, then you may want to wake up from your dream or nightmare and face the unreality of your reality.

UNFAIR TO YOUR LOVER

Why do most women buy into the concept of living with a man without being married? The reason is very simple—

hope. That's right. They hope that one day the man who made numerous vain promises time and time again will suddenly change for the better and make good on his word. I've seen women wait 5, 10, 15, 25, and even 30 years wasting their time waiting for a man to marry them while shacking up with them.

All I could say to them and to myself is how unfair it was to the women who sincerely believed that he would one day walk down the flowered church aisle with her toward the altar to jump over the proverbial broomstick into their nuptial destinies. But instead, my sister, you waited, put it on delay, and prolonged the process. And during the course dozens of *good men* passed you by.

Let me give you a bit of free yet very expensive advice. Don't waste your life waiting for someone to come up to your level. You may literally be waiting a lifetime for that to happen. No matter which way you look at it, that's just not fair to subject someone to, particularly someone you claim to love. True love commits!

If you still want to believe that you should waste your good single life on someone who is unwilling to commit to you in the hope that he or she will someday say "I do," listen to the words of William Bennett in his book, *The Broken Hearth: Reversing the Moral Collapse of the American Family.* He suggests that the hope most people who are cohabiting hope for will probably not happen.

Bennett questions and responds:

Does cohabitation help preserve relationships, as Susan Sarandon asserts? Only about one-sixth of couples who cohabit stay together at least three years, and only one-tenth last five years or more. In other words, for most people, these are inherently unstable arrangements.

This does not mean of course that couples who live together and later marry will inevitably divorce. Nor does it mean that couples who cohabit without marriage cannot live happy and fulfilled lives. Nor does it mean that they cannot raise healthy and productive children. It means, rather that these things are less likely to happen—far less likely to happen—when couples lives together than when they marry.[2]

IMPEDES PROGRESS

Have you ever said to a young person, perhaps a teenager or a pre-teen, "If I could only be your age again, I would have really lived life so much better. I wish I had a second chance to do it all over again." I've even told young people in high school and college as guidance to them: "Enjoy your life now. Live your dreams. Travel the world. Do things that you can do now since you are young that you may not be able to do when you get older." Some young people listen to my counsel while others ignore it, thinking that I am secretly trying to hide something valuable from them. Sad to say, when they choose to ignore my advice they quickly find out that what I was saying was for their benefit, not mine. They then live regretting that they could have listened to me and enjoyed all that life had to offer, but did not.

In the same way, I look at many singles who choose to allow someone to halt their progress, or at least slow it down. To them I say the same thing as I would to an aspiring teenager: "Enjoy your life and live your dreams. Do everything that you always wanted to do. Enjoy your freedom while it lasts." You say, "I thought that marriage was about mutual enjoyment, doing things together and living happily ever after." That is true. However, no two persons always see things quite the same.

Enjoy your life and live your dreams. Do everything that you always wanted to do. Enjoy your singleness while it lasts.

For example, you may desire to go to Australia and your spouse may be adamantly opposed to the idea for whatever reason. Single people don't have to consider those kinds of things. You have a different kind of freedom that is just as beautiful as the freedom that married folks enjoy. You can make power career moves without the possible hindrances of a spouse.

You can do the work of the ministry without having any competition from your spouse, wholly devoting yourself to the cause of Christ and His kingdom. Now, I am not saying that married people are all contentious and bickering and feud over every single decision. I am not trying to portray marriage as a prison sentence. Rather I am trying to convey the truthful message that when you are married or "acting" like you are married, you will always have to consider the other person in virtually everything you do.

That can often slow down the progress of your life. I've seen men who cohabit with women whom they vehemently opposed to getting a college degree, or taking on a new promotion, or traveling the world. He did that because he was intimidated by a woman who was successful. He realized that her success would eventually show up his lack of success and expose his "loserness."

"loserness"
The quality or state of being a loser. This quality can be an inherent, inborn quality or it can be a learned behavioral trait. At times this negative quality may be genetically passed down from one generation to the next. It is a very contagious disease-like quality. Because of that, losers must be avoided at all costs.

There are so many people who would not mind helping you ruin your life since theirs is already ruined. That is why it is so important to pair up with people who are of the same mind and have the same kinds of values. I've seen some of the most beautiful, educated, exuberant, potential-filled women in the world pair up with the most obvious, blatant losers on earth. When I look at them together, I think, *Why in the world would she waste her life with him? Why is she settling for so much less than she deserves? She's outright desperate, and it shows!*

You can do well—all by yourself. You don't have to invite a loser into your life to turn good things into bad ones. Your singleness is a gift from God. It is precious, and you should treasure it for as long as it lasts. Cohabiting not only impedes progress, but it also destroys dreams and possibilities. It averts goals from coming to fruition. It welcomes the sin of procrastination into your life, inevitably dismantling all your successes—past, present, and future. Your life is too precious to waste. Only surround yourself with people, both male and female, who can help you get to where you are going. All others are not invited for the ride.

WHAT ABOUT THE CHILDREN?

Children deserve to be reared in a happy home with a mom and a dad. Although most people never do, they should consider children when making a decision to cohabit. Why should your small child have to view your significant other as a parent when he or she is not? That is unfair to the child. And, it is quite confusing. The most genuine commitment to properly rearing children comes when both parents are married and in agreement concerning the nurture of their children.

Children get awfully confused when they see an erroneous example constantly before them. What's more is that children grow up with a sense of "non-commitment" to anything when they've seen their parents or one of their parents "live together" unmarried all of their life. Although God can change the hearts of humankind, it will take a whole lot of undoing to get a child exposed to that kind of living to understand an "alternative" living arrangement—marriage.

Maybe you have never considered your lifestyle as being a threat or harmful to anyone. The children within your household and those with whom you are in constant contact with deserve to at least know what is righteous from compromising. If you are living in a "live-in" situation that is dishonorable to God, there is no need to beat up on yourself. Simply change. You don't need that other person to help you with the car payment, rent, or groceries. You are much bigger than that. God will provide for you. Your single life is a gift; re-gift life back to yourself and I promise you that you will thank yourself over and again. Do it for God, do it for the children, do it for yourself, do it for your *future*.

TOP TEN REASONS WHY PEOPLE CHOOSE TO COHABIT

1. *Image.* "I have a man. I have a woman. We look like a happy couple."

2. *Fear of being alone.*

3. *Low self-esteem.*

4. *Expectations of marriage.*

5. *Cultural practice.* You've grown up seeing everyone around you doing the same thing.

6. *Peer, family, and societal pressures.* Everyone else is doing it. It's become the common "in" thing to do.

7. *Financial convenience.* Usually one or the other is carrying the weight of financial obligation, while the other one sucks him or her dry.

8. *No commitment* (mostly for men). Easy in, easy out.

9. *Domestic partner seeking insurance benefits.*

10. *Lack of knowledge.* Some folks simply believe that nothing is wrong with it at all.

TOP REASONS WHY PEOPLE SHOULD NOT COHABIT

1. Your freedom is far too important to you.

2. It is too much time to invest and get nothing of value in return.

3. You can be in total control of your own money.

4. You gain the respect of respectable people.

5. You don't have to deal with unnecessary drama, pain, and shame related to non-marital relationships.

6. It can easily obscure the meaning and message of true love.

7. You will not lose your identity in another person but will rather be whole, healthy, and fruitful.

8. You will be different than the world, exemplifying the uniqueness of God.

9. You deserve better than that.

10. You want to be pleasing to God by obeying His Word.

I beseech you therefore, brethren, by the mercies of God, that you present your bodies a living sacrifice, holy, acceptable to God, which is your reasonable service. And do not be conformed to this world, but be transformed by the renewing of your mind, that you may prove what is that good and acceptable and perfect will of God.

Romans 12:1-2

ENDNOTES

1. <http://www.probe.org/docs/e-cohabit.html> April 5, 2005.

2. William Bennett, *The Broken Hearth: Reversing the Moral Collapse of the American Family* (New York: Doubleday, 2001), pp. 77-78.

SINGLE WITH CHILDREN

=⇒●●⇐=

MOMMA AND POPPA DRAMA

"Just marry your baby's daddy no matter what the circumstances may be." If I could get a quarter for every time I heard that statement or one like it said, I'd have at least a thousand bucks by now. Although a single person who has children is not technically single, he or she should still see him or herself as single in the eyes of the Lord. Because of that, you should try to free yourself from any drama that would weaken your witness and your influence in front of your child or children.

I totally believe that a man who makes a baby is obligated by the law and by God's Word to take care of that baby. If there is one thing that totally irks me it is a deadbeat father. In fact, I will always judge a man not by what he has, but rather by how he takes care of his children, particularly if he is not married to the mother of his children. I know of sinners and professing Christian men who live really large, driving Rolls Royces or Mercedes Benz and living in mansions, while their children live in the basement of their grandmother's house. That sickens me.

A man who makes a baby is obligated by the law and by God's Word to take care of that baby.

Personally, I can't understand how a real man could even consider neglecting the kids he helped to create. It seems as if it should be a crime punishable by a life sentence. There is no excuse for it all. I've heard brothers say stuff like, "I'm sick of that woman. She's just trying to bleed me for everything I've got. I earn $800 every week, yet only take home about $175 after child support payments. I can't keep on living like this." To that I say, "Boo hoo. Be a man and take care of your responsibility."

I don't feel any remorse for a man who pays his debt to his children. Who do you suppose should pay for the child's care and provision? Certainly not me or you. Every man should take care of his own responsibility and he should do it with manly pride. I'd be outright embarrassed to have to go to court and stand before a judge waiting to decide what I should give to my child. That is ludicrous. Interestingly enough, most women never know exactly who they gave their bodies to until it's too late.

At times fathers refuse to pay child support to intentionally spite the mother of the child, not considering that the child is the one most affected by his callous actions. Whatever a judge orders a man to pay, he should pay it. Even if he is ordered to get a job or a second job to pay his debt, then he'll have to do just that. Every man should consider work an honor, especially when his work directly benefits his children. Arguing with the child's mother and making stupid agreements and compromises just to evade responsibility is really a futile task. If a man argues why he should not pay, then you must face the fact that you are facing a lost cause. That brings me to my next point.

The sooner you single mothers come to the reality that he is not your source, the quicker God will pour out His provision in your life. The reason God cannot bless you and provide for you as a single mother is because you continue to disgrace Him by allowing your baby's daddy to be His competition. In fact, you've traded God in for him, actually believing that one day he just might become better than God. I've seen time and time again women stop serving God, stop attending church, and cease from giving tithes and offerings, all in the name of pleasing her man. That only lasted until he found another sucker to take for a joy ride, one who had more money to offer than you. Or it came to a quick end when you found out about the other women.

Whatever the case, God was patiently waiting for you to come to your senses and just realize that He was and always has been and always will be your provider. I've already stated how criminal-like and Draconian a deadbeat, non-supportive dad's actions are. However, if that man is not going to take care of his fiscal responsibilities, it is not the end of the world. God desires to make you a financial magnet. He wants to give you witty inventions, creative concepts, and ingenious ideas that will usher you far away from poverty and into your wealthy place.

The only way He can do that, however, is when you choose to put your trust totally in Him and quit chasing a situation that is counterproductive. Stop being the rabbit that continually chases after the carrot that she never gets. Stop trying to get him to do what he never will. And for the men, stop trying to get her to agree with your idiotic, ridiculous actions. Neither you nor she are being compensated for all this Broadway-class drama, so you might as well move on with both of your lives and start seeking out His kingdom and use His methods to get all the stuff you need. That's the only proven method that I know of.

> *But seek first the kingdom of God and His righteousness, and all these things shall be added to you. Therefore do not worry about tomorrow, for tomorrow will worry about its own things. Sufficient for the day is its own trouble.*
>
> Matthew 6:33-34

GOD WILL TAKE CARE OF YOU

So she said, "As the LORD your God lives, I do not have bread, only a handful of flour in a bin, and a little oil in a jar; and see, I am gathering a couple of sticks that I may go in and prepare it for myself and my son, that we may eat it, and die."

1 Kings 17:12

The story of the widow woman at Zarepath is a pristine example of how God will take care of single mothers. No matter how you arrive at being single with children, you are still in the same predicament. This woman in 1 Kings 17 became a single mother after the death of her husband. Unfortunately, her husband left her in debt and did not have any substance or wealth in any form to leave his wife and children as an inheritance.

This left her in a financial hardship. Her son was deathly ill. She only had a little baking flour and some oil to fry some bread with. Just think about it. If this woman thought like many single mothers in our modern age, she would be anxiously searching for a man to take care of her. She would be looking for a strapping, strong, working (or maybe not working) man who would at least give her the illusion that everything would be all right—only to discover a few months down the road that her decision was a bad one.

Not so with this godly woman. This woman did the very thing that always pleases God and gets His attention. What is the thing that always pleases God and gets His attention? The answer to that trivia question is recorded in Hebrews.

But without faith it is impossible to please Him, for he who comes to God must believe that He is, and that He is a rewarder of those who diligently seek Him.

Hebrews 11:6

This woman decided to put her total trust in God. Instead of consuming her last and only meal, she obeyed the prophet Elijah and gave him bread to eat as a firstfruits offering. Sharing her only meal, one that was intended for her and her son, was a remarkable act of faith in God. It was faith and courage in concert that caused God's favor to burst open on her life.

Because she trusted the man of God and did not try to create her miracle by using fleshly means, God opened heaven over her life. Although there was an apparent famine in the land, her flour never dried up and the oil in her cruse continued to replenish itself until the famine was over. This once poor single mother was now able to be a blessing to other people within her community because she believed that God would take care of her.

> *Faith and courage cause God's favor to burst open on your life.*

Her entire story, including subsequent miracles, can be read in the full chapter of 1 Kings 17. I'm sure it will give you a fresh perspective on God's ability to provide for you no matter what your situation may look like. Even today God is using so many single mothers to not only provide for themselves and their children, but also for a host of other people who depend on them for their living.

Michelle Hoskins, the owner of Michelle Foods; author and playwright Maya Angelou; Chicago real estate investor Jaqueline Jackson; anchorwoman and Oprah Winfrey's best friend Gayle King; singer Angie Stone; American Idol Fantasia Barrino; and anthropologist and novelist Zora Neale Hurston are all examples of women who were single yet who provided for their children and many others through the gifts and talents that God bestowed on them. If God could do it for them, then surely He can do it for you too. God is not a respecter of persons; however, He is a respecter of faith. Having children should never be your excuse not to succeed. On the contrary, it should be every reason that you'll ever need to totally and unequivocally believe that God will supply every conceivable need that you will ever have. It all starts with faith.

YOUR CHILD MATTERS MUCH

And when He came near the gate of the city, behold, a dead man was being carried out, the only son of his mother; and she was a widow. And a large crowd from the city was with her. When the Lord saw her, He had compassion on her and said to her, "Do not weep." Then He came and touched the open coffin, and those who carried him stood still. And He said, "Young man, I say to you, arise." So he who was dead sat up and began to speak. And He presented him to his mother. Then fear came upon all, and they glorified God, saying, "A great prophet has risen up among us"; and, "God has visited His people."

Luke 7:12-16

One final reminder to all you precious women with children: Your children should be on the top of your priority list. Never under any circumstance put any man before your children. It is so sad to think of just how many women have actually allowed men to sever ties with their own children. I've seen breaking news stories where women threw their newborn and young babies in the dumpster to comply with their boyfriends' prohibition against children.

Some men have thrown little children out of windows, beat them senseless, and threw them down a flight of stairs while the mother stood by watching. Nothing, and I mean nothing, is more important than your child. In the passage in Luke, Jesus came to the rescue of a mother whose son had died. This woman only had one son. In many ways this son was her one hope, her one friend, her one confidant. Now her child was dead.

Your children should be on the top of your priority list.

Her dreams and hopes of his future had died also. Because of this the woman was tremendously grieved. Jesus, realizing that the woman was so distressed within, had compassion on her and resurrected the child back to life again. In many ways your child is dead too, although he or she may be physically alive. What I mean is that your relationship is so shallow, the time spent together so infrequent, and the genuine interest in his or her well-being so superficial that in many ways it seems to the child as if he or she is not even alive.

God is giving all single mothers a second chance. He is resurrecting relationships gone bad. He is speaking new life back into your parent-child union. For once in your lifetime you are coming to realize that if a man does not love your child, then he is definitely not the one for you. The entire concept of biblical repentance all centers around changing your original thoughts about the sin or transgression that you used to partake in.

Even in the situation of selfishly putting your child in second place or even putting your child at risk or exposing him or her to your lewd behavior, change your mind right now. Purpose in your heart that from this very moment, you will treasure the gift (your child) that God has given you.

You will not expose your child to illicit behavior but rather cover him or her from worldly influences until the child is of an age when he or she can fend for him or herself.

Finally, if you've forgotten before, you will make it a high priority to never again forget that your child matters and that his or her overall well-being should come before any of your selfish or fleshly desires. Change your mind, change your actions, change your world, and you will receive better results.

Chapter Eight

THE PROCESS OF WAITING

But those who wait on the LORD shall renew their strength; they shall mount up with wings like eagles, they shall run and not be weary, they shall walk and not faint.

Isaiah 40:31

We live in a microwave generation. Everywhere you look you'll find people who want goods and services in a hurry. McDonalds delivers a cheeseburger in less than a minute. Jiffy Lube will have your oil changed in your car within ten minutes guaranteed. FedEx will have your package delivered overnight to any domestic location. I suppose that the conventional way Blockbuster video rental operated in the past wasted far too much time for most Americans, which engendered the birth of NetFlix® where you never have to leave home at all. DVDs are delivered right to your door. Even your email is delivered in an instant because sending a message via the traditional U.S. Postal Service just does not work for those really burning memorandums.

This same mind-set has been fostered in the hearts of many singles. "When will he or she come?" you ask with such anxious anticipation. But really the right question should rather be, "What can I benefit during this intimate time between God and me?" There are valuable benefits to waiting. Isaiah gave a special insight even to singles on what you can expect to receive as a result of your waiting.

There are four things you can expect to receive while waiting.

1. *Renewed strength.* Believe me when I tell you that there are a whole lot of temptations as well as major distractions in the world, enough for any single person to get involved in. If you are going to win this battle against secularism and worldly interest, you are going to need God's strength. The number one problem with us singles is when we try to be strong without the help of the Lord, when we rely on our own strength. God's strength is made perfect and becomes very obvious in our weakness. However, His strength will only begin to manifest in our life at the onset of our waiting.

2. *God-given power to soar like the eagles.* Have you ever been to a doctor's or a dentist's office for a visit? I'm sure you have. In the waiting room you'll often see magazines made available to you for your read-

ing pleasure while you wait. It's just one of the things that you need to help you pass the time without being bored to death. Well, God also has a few perks while you wait. However, His perks are far more elaborate than a magazine or some cappuccino and donuts. God literally empowers you to become like an eagle. You will be elevated in your process of waiting. The interesting thing is that as you become more and more patient in your waiting process, after a while it won't even seem like you are waiting anymore—particularly since you will have a God-given ability to soar way above your problems, your challenges, and your shortcomings to a place you never dreamed existed, one prepared especially for you by your Father.

3. *Ability to run without ever getting tired.* Personally, I am always trying to stay conscious of my need to exercise on a regular basis. Although I feel like I am in pretty good shape, I still have the propensity to tire out quickly when I am running. I realize that the race that is set before me can be far more tiresome than running around a high school track four or five times. God's Word informs me that while I wait, I will be able to run and run and continue on running without getting tired. What an encouragement. If I choose to get married it won't be because I got tired of being single, but rather because I found someone who was running the same race with me and was suitable for me.

4. *Capable of walking without ever experiencing weakness.* When I don't feel like running, then I'll walk. But if I go into my cool-down stage, I can expect to receive

supernatural power that will enable me not to experience the slightest signs of weakness. While you wait expect to be empowered, expect to learn from your journey, and expect to win over and again.

I wait for the LORD, my soul waits, and in His word I do hope. My soul waits for the Lord more than those who watch for the morning—yes, more than those who watch for the morning.

Psalm 130:5-6

AIN'T NO NEED TO HURRY

Now Laban had two daughters; the name of the older was Leah, and the name of the younger was Rachel. Leah had weak eyes, but Rachel was lovely in form, and beautiful. Jacob was in love with Rachel and said, "I'll work for you seven years in return for your younger daughter Rachel." Laban said, "It's better that I give her to you than to some other man. Stay here with me." So Jacob served seven years to get Rachel, but they seemed like only a few days to him because of his love for her. Then Jacob said to Laban, "Give me my wife. My time is completed, and I want to lie with her."

Genesis 29:16-21 NIV

When morning came, there was Leah! So Jacob said to Laban, "What is this you have done to me? I served you for Rachel, didn't I? Why have you deceived me?" Laban replied, "It is not our custom here to give the younger daughter in marriage before the older one. Finish this daughter's bridal week; then we will give you the younger one also, in return for another seven years of work." And Jacob did so. He finished the week with Leah, and then Laban gave him his daughter Rachel to be his wife. Laban gave his servant girl Bilhah to his daughter Rachel as her maidservant. Jacob lay with Rachel also, and he loved Rachel more than Leah. And he worked for Laban another seven years.

Genesis 29:25-30 NIV

This narrative is a particularly comical one—well, probably not for Jacob. Jacob was an eligible bachelor who wanted to get married to the woman of his dreams. He, like so many of us today, made the grave mistake of sizing up a potential partner by her exterior package only. He thought that Rachel was very beautiful and on that alone he decided to pursue her interest.

Come to find out, this young lady was well worth her price. Jacob would eventually pay the high price of having to marry her older sister first, work and wait a total of 14 years, then marry his dream bride Rachel. How many people today do you suppose would have waited 14 years without having sexual intercourse to marry the man or woman of their dreams? Okay, that's a dumb question with an obvious answer. However, I hope you are getting my point.

Our generation is not even conditioned to wait for a bride or groom. There are so many unassuming women who rush into marriage only to discover later that they married a boy rather than a man simply because they were unwilling to wait for the "Boys to Turn to Men." You've probably heard the adage, "You will get what you pay for." I believe that based on this situation you will get in life what you are willing to wait for.

Are T.D. Jakes, Joyce Meyers, Mother Teresas, Joel Osteens, and Billy Grahams birthed in a moment's time? Absolutely not! Each one of these spiritual giants was born and grew to maturity on the backside of the desert hidden from the real world until the time of their season had fully come. Far too many people run into a ministry before it's their time. Businesses fail every single day because somebody wasn't willing to wait and learn the rules of the game. People lose deposits on property because the timing was wrong for purchasing property. It bothers me that people are just unwilling to wait.

You will get in life what you are willing to wait for.

There is really no need to hurry, especially as it relates to relationships. Live your life to the fullest. Thoroughly evaluate all newcomers. Know in the core of your heart that anything that is really valuable in life is going to take time in order to acquire. You've been willing to wait to get a degree, to find the right home, to receive your pension and social security. Wouldn't it make sense to wait for the right mate? You ask, "Suppose I wait for a lifetime. Then what?"

If you even waited for a lifetime to avoid the wrong one, you've still done well. Who wants to be miserable just to say that they've got somebody in their life? I want God's choice for me, one that I know will last. And, if that package doesn't come to my doorstep tomorrow morning or even next week,

I'll be all right. I'm in no hurry. I'm enjoying this process of waiting.

MR. & MRS. RIGHT?—WRONG

There is no such thing as Mr. & Mrs. Right. The better idea is Mr. & Mrs. "Working on Becoming Right." That is the whole process of life. We are always becoming. And in our becoming we discover true happiness. The whole ideology of Mr. & Mrs. Right is really a fallacy, a fairy tale at best. What most people call right and wrong are usually based on looks and style far more than on character and integrity anyway. Furthermore, what's right for you may not be right for me, and vice versa. You may have a certain style that does not vibe well with me at all. Make it far more important to you to have the right fit rather than the right appearance. Looks really are deceiving.

CHARACTER COUNTS

Character counts more than we are sometimes willing to admit. I have friendships with people. At this point in my life, "I've been there and done that" and I am not really looking for anything more than God's purposes being fulfilled in my life. So in the meantime, while that is happening, I need the right team of people around me. I need to be around people who have values, people who are goal-oriented, and people of purpose.

I don't even have a second to waste. Honestly, I don't really have time to make a whole bunch of new friends; I already have enough. So at this point, I can be very selective about who comes into my life and who I want to kick off the boat. If you don't have character, then there is no need to apply. I have waited patiently and happily too long in life to allow some idiot to mess up everything that I've worked hard to build.

What are you made of? How do you respond under intense pressure? What is your philosophy on life? What principles do you live by? Where are you going? The answers to all those questions will better help me to determine what kind of character you actually are. I can find out what kind of character you are in a few minutes. But it may take a while for me to find out what kind of character you possess. It's worth the wait.

WHAT ARE YOUR VALUES?

What do you value? One of the things that I have come to know in life is that we don't get what we want in life always. But we always attract what we value. The truth is that if you don't know what you value, then you are an easy target for an assault. You have to know what you value and what you really want in life and from people. That should be a part of the vision for your life. And your vision should be easily articulated and written down if it will ever come to fruition.

> *Then the LORD answered me and said: "Write the vision and make it plain on tablets, that he may run who reads it."*
>
> Habakkuk 2:2

Right now write down five things that you value most in life. Whatever those things are, whomever comes into your life should have the same values. If they do not, then they are not compatible for your friendship. After that write down five things that you want (expect) out of life. You need to see in writing exactly what your values are. It may amaze you when you actually see it in writing. Go ahead—start thinking and write!

Five Things That I Value Most

1.

2.

3.

4.

5.

Five Things That I Desire in Life

1.

2.

3.

4.

5.

LEARNING FROM PAST MISTAKES

I always use my past failures and mistakes as a guide to my success. With all my heart, I try not to ever make the same mistake twice. That is one worthwhile attribute about waiting in life. I've learned that the deal of a lifetime comes every day. The "right one" is really not going away any time soon. Whoever God designed for me won't work well with anyone else.

I have made so many mistakes along my journey. There is one thing that I am eternally grateful for, and that is the forgiving power of God. God has forgiven me and covered me through some of the most tumultuous storms. Looking back, I sometimes wondered how I made it even to this point in life of being able to share with you. All I can truthfully say is that it was nobody but Jesus.

At the same time, there are two things I have committed to do in life. First, I am committed to learning the valuable lessons from every past mistake of mine. Second, I am committed to gaining knowledge from valuable lessons learned through other people's mistakes. I don't have to get hit by a bus, fall off of an icy mountain, run into a burning house with fierce flames, or lose all my money on the stock market if you first do it for me.

I say that somewhat facetiously, but I'm really serious. I can learn not only from my mistakes, but also from yours. And learning from your mistakes is far less costly and hurtful for me. Some things in life I cannot avoid; they are inevitable. Then there are the mistakes that I could have easily avoided had I taken the time to see the handwriting on the wall in large graffiti bold print. Learn from your past mistakes and grow.

To err is human; but human error easily slips into three crimes; the initial mistake becomes deliberate wrong; attempt is then made to cure the wrong by force rather than reason; finally the whole story is so explained and distorted as to preserve no lesson for posterity, and thus history seldom guide us aright.[1]

ENDNOTE

1. W.E.B. Du Bois, Foreword to *Freedom Road*, 1969, as cited in Dorothy Wimbush Riley, ed., *My 'Soul Looks Back, 'Less I Forget: A Collection of Quotations By People of Color* (New York: Harper Collins, 1993), p. 271.

Chapter Nine

THE BENEFITS OF BEING SINGLE

———⊱⊰———

I would like you to be free from concern. An unmarried man is concerned about the Lord's affairs—how he can please the Lord. But a married man is concerned about the affairs of this world—how he can please his wife—and his interests are divided. An unmarried woman or virgin is concerned about the Lord's affairs: Her aim is to be devoted to the Lord in both body and spirit. But a married woman is concerned about the affairs of this world—how she can please her husband. I am saying this for your own good, not to restrict you, but that you may live in a right way in undivided devotion to the Lord.

1 Corinthians 7:32-35 NIV

BRINGS PLEASURE TO GOD

Based on this scripture passage it is fairly obvious that the most important reason a person would choose to be single is not really a self-centered motive. Singles should choose to be single so that they can please the Lord. Now understand the phrase *"please the Lord."* This phrase does not suggest that if you are married or contemplating marriage that you are displeasing to God. We all know that God desires people to rear godly families.

Singles who operate in faith bring God the highest amount of pleasure.

The context that this *"please the Lord"* is actually set in, is from the perspective of Hebrews 11:6, which states, *"But without faith it is impossible to please Him, for he who comes to God must believe that He is, and that He is a rewarder of those who diligently seek Him."* Again you can see the word *please* in this verse. It is in this regard that single people have a potential advantage over their married counterparts. As children of God, when you operate in faith, you bring God the highest amount of pleasure.

Your faith does not have to go through a checkmate-type of system. God speaks to your heart and you simply do what you believe God told you to do. It's as simple as that. You don't have to take a vote or get familial opinions or solicit advice from your family members. At a moment's notice you can go where God desires for you to go. To God, that level of faith response is quite important.

I believe that God really wants to bless singles even in the area of finances. For far too long, particularly many single women (obviously not all) have waited around for a man to take care of all their needs. There is nothing inherently wrong with a man who chooses to take full care of women. However, too many men play childish games, making the women do ridiculous things in order to receive the favor of financial provision in return. I say, "It's just not worth it."

In the time that you use to worry over him, you can easily start a business, go back to school, create an invention, invest your money, and watch the unusually spectacular results happen. The reason I mentioned all those things is to show you that God needs a vehicle through which He can communicate His blessings. So college, business, investing, and creative ideas are all vehicles that will inevitably transfer wealth into your hands if you are properly connected.

All this only happens by faith, though. Let me go a bit further. Have you ever seen a husband and wife, one born again, the other not? In that type of situation it is so hard for the couple to ever receive optimal blessings since they are not in agreement. Things only happen in the positive or negative sense when two people are in agreement. From that point of view, it is better to be alone rather than to force a disagreeable person to try to be on the same playing field with you. The lack of disagreement, the strife, and the grief all cause confusion—an environment that God cannot work in. So this brings ultimate displeasure to the Father. Most singles can at least agree with themselves. At least I hope so.

FREES YOU UP TO DO THE WORK OF THE MINISTRY

What exactly is ministry anyway? Most people immediately think of church, a pulpit, and an enthusiastic minister preaching away when one mentions the word *ministry*. Although that is obviously ministry, ministry is not limited to the four walls of the church. Ministry should begin in the house of the Lord but extend to the four corners of the earth. So ministry then is responding to the command of God to use your gifts, talents, time, and resources to benefit the needs of mankind.

From that definition there is a whole lot of people whom we can include on the list of ministers, people who are devoted to communicate God's help and love in some special way. Mother Teresa was a minister. She selflessly ministered the unconditional love of the Lord Jesus Christ to poor hurting children in Calcutta, India, and for that she will receive a great heavenly reward.

> *And God is able to make all grace abound to you, so that in all things at all times, having all that you need, you will abound in every good work. As it is written: "He has scattered abroad his gifts to the poor; his righteousness endures forever." Now he who supplies seed to the sower and bread for food will also supply and increase your store of seed and will enlarge the harvest of your righteousness. You will be made rich in every way so that you can be generous on every occasion, and through us your generosity will result in thanksgiving to God.*
>
> 2 Corinthians 9:8-11 NIV

The Bible gives us clear mandates to minister to the needs of the poor, as well as to *"every good work."* Oprah Winfrey is perhaps the single most influential female philanthropist in the world. She is a help to the world. And because of her contribution through television and communications, she is instrumental in making the world a better place to live in.

Comedian and playwright and brainchild behind the movie *Diary of a Mad Black Woman*, Tyler Perry is a minister of healing especially in the sense that he makes people laugh through his acting. The Bible tells us that a merry heart can have therapeutic attributes. I know firsthand how many times I personally needed a good laugh simply to relieve unwanted stress. The funny thing is, that laughing worked. Although he is not in the pulpit preaching Sunday after Sunday, that does not diminish his effectiveness at all.

You can do more ministry, more helping folks, and even more giving when you are single.

A merry heart does good, like medicine, but a broken spirit dries the bones.

Proverbs 17:22

There are so many people—both male and female—whom God is using mightily in the areas of business, sports, entertainment, music, the arts, literature, law and politics, and almsgiving who are ministers of His grace. According to the apostle Paul, you can do more ministry, more helping folks, and even more giving when you are single. You can devote your total self wholeheartedly to the purpose of the ministry whether it is literally preaching and teaching God's Word or being used in the other various ways that I mentioned.

Although the wife, husband, and children are all a wonderful thing, they will compete for your time, resources, and attention, thus limiting your overall effectiveness in the area of your ministry to others. Us single folks don't worry about that. That is why we are a rare and valuable commodity, especially when we know our truest value to God and humanity. Those are perhaps the top reasons for remaining single since God and His people are both high priorities. However, there are a few other reasons that may not chart as high on the list as God, His church, and His people, but that nonetheless matter to most singles.

OTHER REASONS FOR THE TRULY SINGLE

- More personal freedom is the best bonus of being single.

- Having my home in the order that I want it in all the time.

- Don't have to answer to anyone other than God and His delegated spiritual representatives.

- The ability to choose exactly what I want. And if I don't get it, then I don't have to live with it.

Interestingly, a recent survey listed the top qualities that males and females desired their potential partner to have. Notice that on the third quality men and women were in major disagreement—not so good a sign.

TOP QUALITIES BOTH MALE AND FEMALE SINGLES WANT IN A NEW PARTNER

- Pleasing personality/sense of humor (67%)

- Common interests and activities (49%)

- Oops, the sexes disagree on this one. Women look for similar moral or religious values (39%), while guys want a woman who's great looking (40%)[1]

Hear, O Israel: The LORD our God, the LORD is one. Love the LORD your God with all your heart and with all your soul and with all your strength.

Deuteronomy 6:4-5 NIV

Probably the most important thing Christian singles love about their singleness is that they can love God wholly and freely. That alone is well worth it all.

I'd like to end with a very special poem written by poet Paul Hughes that embodies the heart of God's expectation for singleness. I hope that each of my words has encouraged you to live at a higher level of awareness and appreciation for the gift of singleness that God has given you. As I travel around the country conducting seminars and workshops on this topic, I would greatly appreciate meeting you face to face, if time permits. But there is one thing that you must promise me: When you see me face to face, you have to admit that ever since you read this book that you have been "living single and loving it!"

LONELINESS

Being alone does not mean I am weak

Though embedded in many hearts

But loneliness is a state of mind a daily struggle

A constant fight within

When no one drops in

To extend a reassuring word

Or listen to my redundant rhetoric,

Of being engaged in singleness.

A lent ear, a pure caress,

A grin to save the day

Helps fight the anguish of loneliness

The fear of singleness itself

For singles exist everywhere

Some feel as if they've been cursed

And the only one who can dispel it

Is a friend who is willing first.[2]

ENDNOTES

1. Linda Fisher, Xenia Montenegro, Research Directors; Sonya Gross, Sarah Mahoney, Tracy Needham, Contributors. <http://www.aarp-magazine.org/people/Articles/a2003-09-23-survey_results.html> April 5, 2005.

2. Copyright ©2005 by Genella Milner. Used with permission.

ABOUT THE AUTHOR

———⊳•◁———

Kervin J. Smith is an international conference speaker, teacher, motivational speaker, lecturer, and consultant. He is the founder and president of Kervin J. Smith Ministries.

The preaching and teaching ministry of Kervin J. Smith is unique, scholarly, life-changing, and relevant to everyday issues. His is a ministry called to reach people with a message of hope through Jesus Christ and embracing one's spiritual and prophetic destiny.

He travels around the world and is known for his keen and accurate prophetic insight, expository teaching, and powerful healing ministry. His ministry crosses denominational lines and transcends racial barriers. Kervin J. Smith has been given a strong mandate from the Lord to provide a clear prophetic voice to the body of Christ.

He has been invited to be a speaker in various venues, including churches, universities, and corporations. He also has been a visiting professor at several universities. He has ministered to government officials, celebrities, professional athletes, and high-level executives in Fortune 500 companies. Kervin J. Smith also has been featured on many syndicated talk shows, radio forums, and symposiums, including the Trinity Broadcasting Network (TBN).

If you would like to schedule Kervin J. Smith for a speaking engagement, contact:

Kervin J. Smith
P.O. Box 46401
Eden Prairie, MN 55344
E-mail: kervinjsmithmin@aol.com
Phone: (201) 681-0706

OTHER BOOKS
BY THE AUTHOR

―――➤●◄―――

Body Building: Getting the Church in Shape

Prophetic Power

Understanding the Three Types of Anointing

Jezebel's Church

What about false Promises?

Chapter 1

A man has to ~~be~~ meet your mental, Emotional
Spiritual and financial requirement.

    pg 16

    Pg 36 It is not about your past, but your present

    pg 40, 48

LK 10 v 19 * Psalm 119 vs 73

    Pg 58 tragenic dating

    60 Dating believers

Personal Journal

Personal Journal

_____

_____

_____

_____

_____

_____

_____

_____

_____

_____

_____

_____

_____

_____

_____

_____

_____

_____

_____

_____

_____

_____

_____

_____

_____

Personal Journal